mental_floss presents

instant
knowledge

Also available from mental_flos

mental_floss presents

instant
knowledge

Edited by

WILL PEARSON

and

MANGESH HATTIKUDUR

🔾 **Collins**

An Imprint of HarperCollins*Publishers*

HarperCollins books may be purchased for educational,
business, or sales promotional use. For information please
write: Special Markets Department, HarperCollins
Publishers, 10 East 53rd Street, New York, NY 10022.

FIRST EDITION

Designed by William Ruoto

ISBN-10 0-06-083461-7
ISBN-13 978-0-06-083461-6

05 06 07 08 09 ❖/WOR 10 9 8 7 6 5 4 3 2 1

— FOR IMMEDIATE RELEASE —

from mental_floss specialty roasters, inc.

Dear Consumer:

We're happy to tell you that you can still get knowledge the old way. mental_floss will always be the family-owned company you can trust for those delicious, slow-roasted facts you've grown to love. But after numerous taste tests and focus groups, we've realized that there's an even better way to serve our most active readers—the ones rushing straight from one draining conversation to the next. Whether you're racing to a cocktail party or the water cooler, a poker game or a United Nations bake sale (you know who you are, Kofi!), mental_floss's *Instant Knowledge* is a full-bodied jolt for thirsty minds on the go.

Best of all, mental_floss has made sure that these rich blends are ready in seconds. Just look over the A–Z, tear into a topic of your choice, and add conversation. It's that simple! And if you need a little guidance on how best to use these facts (who you'll be able to impress or where best to drop your newfound knowledge), we've provided that, too.

Just look to the icons for help! If you're in a pinch at a

cocktail party, while trying to console a friend, or even desperate to make small talk (at a funeral, no less!), we've got a fact for you. Just search the icons for a stick figure in your situation, and you'll find the perfect words for your dilemma. Oh, and we've provided some keywords, too. If you happen to hear one of them in passing, go ahead and spill your knowledge. You'll be glad you did.

So, go ahead and sample a few right now. Skim a few pages, dip into a few facts, and see if you can still taste that robust mental_floss flavor in every delicious sip.

Bottoms Up,

Will and Mangesh

THE AMISH

(especially those fond of the "devil's dandruff")

USEFUL FOR: cocktail parties, whenever the electricity goes out, and anytime you're in Lancaster, Pennsylvania

KEYWORDS: bikers, buggies, or blow

THE FACT: Amish youths experiencing some requisite angst have plenty of ways to rebel (like oh, say, flipping on a light switch!), but these two guys really went above and beyond.

In June 1998, two members of the conservative Old Order Amish sect in Pennsylvania were arrested for buying and selling cocaine. The men, *both* named Abner Stoltzfus but *not* related, had apparently been riding their horse and buggy to meet up with a motorcycle gang known as the Pagans (seriously) and then distributing cocaine at their community hoedowns (honestly, we're not making this stuff up). Between 1993 and 1997, the wild and crazy pair reportedly purchased over $100,000 worth of cocaine.

ANTIBIOTICS

(a.k.a. Chicken Throat for the Soul)

USEFUL FOR: waiting rooms, chatting up scientists, and hitting on pharmacists

KEYWORDS: penicillin, Alexander Fleming, or chickens

THE FACT: Believe it or not, biologist Selman Waksman discovered a revolutionary antibiotic in the back of a chicken's throat.

In the 1930s, Selman Waksman, working at Rutgers University, became interested in isolating antibiotics from fungi, hoping to find another "penicillin." To aid his quest, he asked his colleagues to send him samples of any unusual species they encountered. One day a farmer came to see a Rutgers veterinarian with a sick chicken in tow. All of his chickens, he said, were suffering from the same kind of disease as the sample. The vet found that the bird had a fungal throat infection, and remembering Waksman's request, he sent him a throat swab. From a culture of this fungus, Waksman eventually isolated streptomycin, an antibiotic that revolutionized the treatment of infections, particularly tuberculosis. So the next time you've got strep throat, make sure to thank a chicken for the cure.

APPETITES

(for construction)

USEFUL FOR: making small talk at the salad bar

KEYWORDS: iron stomach, all you can eat, or I'm so hungry I could eat a plane

THE FACT: Looking for inspiration when trying to down your mother-in-law's meat loaf? Just consider the story of Michel Lotito, the French gent who once ate an entire Cessna 150.

Yes, that's an entire plane we're talking about, and the guy who did it goes by the nickname Monsieur Mangetout (French for "eats everything." See what he did there?). Lotito engaged in the stunt to earn a place in the *Guinness World Records* (his actual record is for the Strangest Diet: 2 pounds of metal per day), but his iron stomach's downed a lot more than just a plane. He's the proud eater of 18 bicycles, a bunch of TVs, a wooden coffin, and several supermarket shopping carts. Not to mention all the lightbulbs, razor blades, and other knickknacks he's downed on variety shows. Looking for a reason why you shouldn't try this at home (or with your home)? Well, Lotito's got a natural advantage because his stomach lining is twice as thick as a normal person's. He's also aided by the fact that he's French, which means he'll eat just about anything if prepared right (escargot, anyone?).

ARITHMETIC

(you're not the only one who hates it)

USEFUL FOR: irritating your math teacher, impressing your (other) liberal arts profs, or just plain comforting anyone who hates math

KEYWORDS: asymptote, parabola, or quadratic equations

THE FACT: Despite the fact that it can be applied to just about everything, there's still no Nobel Prize given out for mathematics.

When dynamite inventor (that's not a comment on his abilities; he really did invent dynamite) Alfred Nobel stipulated in his will that his fortune be used to establish a fund to award five annual prizes "to those who, during the preceding year, shall have conferred the greatest benefit on mankind," he mysteriously left out math. And all kinds of theories have popped up to explain the omission, most of which claim that Nobel hated all mathematicians because his wife was schtupping one on the side. Nope. The most likely reasons for Nobel's ditching math are 1) He simply didn't like math all that much, and 2) Sweden already had a big, fancy prize for mathematics, from the journal *Acta Mathematica*. Although math is still a Nobel bridesmaid, a prize for economics was added in 1968, thereby giving the extremely boring sciences their due.

ASPARAGUS

(and your tee-tee)

USEFUL FOR: cocktail parties, explaining yourself at the urinal, and chatting up people from the Philadelphia Historical Society

KEYWORDS: kites, Ben Franklin or "I really, really have to powder my nose"

THE FACT: Who would have guessed that the genius who figured out that asparagus and unscented urine don't always go together was none other than Ben Franklin?

Benjamin Franklin made many contributions to science, including bifocals, the Franklin stove, and lightning rods. But he was also the first to record that some people produced urine with a disagreeable odor after eating asparagus. You'll be grateful to know that the smell has now been identified and due to sulfur-containing compounds produced when asparagus is metabolized. It seems, however, that not everyone can generate these compounds. A study examined the urine of 115 people who dined on the green vegetable, and only 46 produced the smell. Strangely, not everyone can smell it either.

ATTILA

("the honey pie")

USEFUL FOR: cocktail parties, wakes, and proving too much lovin' will actually kill a barbarian

KEYWORDS: lucky, truly blessed, or what a way to go

THE FACT: Attila the Hun, history's perennial bad boy, was apparently also a perennial playboy. In fact, the guy actually died in the act.

The leader of the Huns, Attila somehow also found time to marry 12 women and father an unknown number of children. Despite his insatiable appetite, though, Attila probably should have kept that last relationship platonic. After all, it was on his wedding night in 453 CE that the middle-aged Hun burst an artery while celebrating his most recent installment of conjugal bliss. Burying him with vast treasures for the afterlife, his followers reportedly ensured that grave robbers would never find his burial place by diverting a tributary of the Danube, burying the body (in a gold coffin inside a silver coffin inside a lead coffin) under the exposed riverbed, and then diverting the water back to its original course to cover it. Of course, the captives who buried him were all killed afterward.

THE BABE

(a.k.a. the Sultan of Swat, the King of Crash)

USEFUL FOR: ballpark chatter, seventh-inning stretches, and anytime you're watching *The Sandlot*

KEYWORDS: Sultan of Swat, King of Crash, Great Bambino, etc.

THE FACT: Home wasn't the only plate at which George Herman "Babe" Ruth was a dominator.

This guy had a big appetite for everything—food, drink, women, you name it. In fact, the Sultan of Swat's favorite breakfast was said to include a porterhouse steak, six fried eggs, and potatoes, all washed down with a quart mixture of bourbon whiskey and ginger ale. The Babe also had a certain fondness for hot dogs, downing between 12 and 18 one day in April 1925. Disgustingly enough, one of the Babe's partially eaten hot dogs (now black and shriveled and nasty) is still on display at the Baseball Reliquary in Monrovia, California. And although Ruth became pretty hefty in the last few years of his career, the rumor that the Yankees adopted their famous pinstripes to make him look slimmer is false. The pinstripes first appeared in 1912, when the Yanks were still the New York Highlanders.

BABY FOOD

(now for eligible adults!)

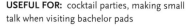

USEFUL FOR: cocktail parties, making small talk when visiting bachelor pads

KEYWORDS: single, singles, or what's worse than New Coke?

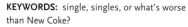

THE FACT: No matter how well known your brand is, there are some markets you just can't tap into . . . like trying to pitch baby food as grown-up chow.

At some point in time, almost every adult has tasted baby food and discovered that the stuff isn't half bad. But that doesn't mean people want to make a meal out of it. For some reason, Gerber had to learn that lesson the hard way. In 1974, the company released Gerber Singles, small servings of food meant for single adults, packaged in jars that were almost identical to those used for baby food. It didn't take long for Gerber execs to figure out that most consumers, unless they were under a year old, couldn't get used to eating a pureed meal out of a jar—particularly one depressingly labeled "Singles." Baby food for grown-ups was pulled from the marketplace shortly after its birth.

BABY JUMPING

USEFUL FOR: baby showers, first birthdays, and making small talk at track-and-field events

KEYWORDS: jump, baby, or please jump my baby

THE FACT: In parts of northern Spain, newborns take part in a ceremony that's disturbingly similar to an Evel Knievel stunt.

Several babies are placed on a mattress surrounded by members of the community while a man jumps over the length of the mattress. (We're thinking they must have professional baby leapers over there.) The ceremony is based on the biblical story in which King Herod ordered all male babies in the area to be killed after hearing that a "new king" had been born in Bethlehem. Just as Mary and Joseph escaped with baby Jesus to Egypt, this Spanish ritual is meant to symbolize a similar experience for a child. By undergoing this and coming out unharmed, the babies are prepared for a safe passage through childhood.

BABY NAMES

(. . . you might not want to give your kid)

USEFUL FOR: baby showers, making friends at Lamaze, and justifying your lack of preparation at your kid's birth

KEYWORDS: curses, spirits, or *The Exorcist*

THE FACT: Since many societies believe that newborns are particularly susceptible to evil spirits, a baby's name is sometimes kept secret (or not given at all) so it can't be used against the child in spells.

In some Haitian, Nigerian, and Romany (Gypsy) cultures, babies are given two names at the time of birth. The parents keep one of them a secret, and they do not share it with the child until he is considered old enough to guard the name for himself. Similarly, in Thailand, a newborn is often referred to by a nickname (usually that of an animal or a descriptive term) to escape the attention of evil spirits, who are believed to be the spirits of dead, childless, unmarried women. The newborn is given a two-syllable name that is mainly used later on by teachers, employers, and during formal occasions. Some Vietnamese parents even delay naming their baby until it's over one month old—the safety margin, spiritwise.

BAD TRADES

(how Cincinnati gets hosed)

USEFUL FOR: ballpark chatter, seventh-inning stretches, impressing anyone over the age of 100 (who still remembers baseball)

KEYWORDS: bad trades, bad management, or bad foresight

THE FACT: Forget the Curse of the Bambino. Compared to this gaffe by the Cincinnati Reds, Boston's decision to trade Babe Ruth (and the subsequent 86-year curse) looks like a carefully orchestrated work of managerial genius.

In 1900, the Reds traded relative newcomer and Renaissance man Christopher "Christy" Mathewson to the New York Giants for the ailing "Hoosier Thunderbolt," Amos Rusie. Following this brilliant move, Mathewson won 372 games for the Giants, including more than 20 games in 11 different seasons. He won wide renown as one of the greatest pitchers in baseball history. Rusie, on the other hand, pitched in three games following the trade, losing one and winning none . . . following which he promptly retired.

BANK ROBBERY

(gone wrong)

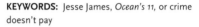

USEFUL FOR: cocktail parties, road trips, chatting up your bank teller

KEYWORDS: Jesse James, *Ocean's 11,* or crime doesn't pay

THE FACT: Despite a ridiculously well known cast of rascals, the Great Northfield, Minnesota Raid was one of the worst-executed heists in history.

It's true, in terms of actual success this robbery was a total bust. But just take a peek at the culprits: legendary bandits Frank and Jesse James; Cole, Jim, and Bob Younger; and three lesser-known outlaws. Their target was Northfield's First National Bank, which the gang settled on after casing a half-dozen other towns. Clearly, not enough casing, as the robbery couldn't have gone worse. The bank's cashier refused to open the safe, an alert passerby sounded the alarm, and townspeople killed two of the robbers as the rest escaped. A week later, a posse killed or captured all of the other outlaws except the James brothers, who escaped home to Missouri. It was the beginning of the end for 19th-century America's most notorious bandits. Worse still? The entire take from the Northfield bank was a mere $26.70.

BEARDS

(a.k.a. The Trouble with Stubble)

USEFUL FOR: cocktail parties, chatting up cat lovers, and questioning the Amish and other assorted bearded folk

KEYWORDS: beard, stubble, or chin whiskers

THE FACT: If you're having trouble relating to your cat, perhaps you should think about shaving.

A study led by Fairfield University indicates that cats react negatively to men with long, dark beards. On the other hand, the fickle felines seem rather indifferent to short beards or unshaven men. In another study, Robert Bork's distinctive partial beard caused disorientation and paralysis in some cats. Of course, now all we need is a study to figure out *why* cats don't like facial hair. It will probably require a hefty chunk of grant money, but we're certain it would be worth it.

instant personalities

PABLO PICASSO liked to carry around a Browning revolver loaded with blanks just so he could fire it at any bourgeois who asked him what his work meant. (Talk about a loaded question!)

American icon **WALT DISNEY** loved tomato juice so much that he offered it to everyone who came to his office . . . and got seriously upset if they didn't drink it!

Despite the fact that propaganda pics always had him showing off his pearly whites, **CHAIRMAN MAO TSE-TUNG** was actually pretty lax with his dental hygiene, and often reasoned: "If tigers don't brush their teeth, why should I?"

BERTRAND RUSSELL

(the Cambridge Casanova)

USEFUL FOR: academic gatherings, impressing professors, and giving philosophy majors hope

KEYWORDS: philosophy, Russell, or The Ladies Man

THE FACT: One of the founders of analytic philosophy, at first blush Bertrand Russell sounds like a pretty dry guy. But you don't get a nickname like the Cambridge Casanova by staying in on Friday nights.

Bertrand Russell had been orphaned at a young age, but before his father died, he instructed that young Bertie be raised agnostic—a decision that no doubt had some impact on the philosopher's life. Plagued by bouts of depression as a young man, Russell quickly learned to cultivate a zest for life. In fact, this heavy-drinking, pipe-smoking professor was notorious for having affairs with his friends' wives (on top of his four attempts at marriage!). He lived passionately, rejecting organized religion with his famous essay "Why I Am Not a Christian," but spent his life pursuing social justice. He even flirted with runs for political office and did jail time for political protest (his last stint being at age 94!). Most notably, perhaps, Russell was a leading intellectual voice against nuclear weapons and the war in Vietnam.

BLACKJACK

(or playing your cards right MIT-style)

USEFUL FOR: cocktail parties, MIT reunions, and chatting up anyone who loves that *Dogs Playing Poker* picture

KEYWORDS: blackjack, Vegas, or the phrase "the geeks shall inherit the earth"

THE FACT: Most people say the house always wins, but in the 1990s there was good reason to put your money on MIT.

Blackjack is a beatable game—that is, if you can count cards well enough to know when the deck favors the player, not the house. And while solitary card counters are relatively easy to spot for most casino security outfits, it took them six years during the 1990s to tumble to the strategy used by a group of MIT students. Using card-counting *teams*, complete with diversionary players—the cavalier math-letes raked in millions. One player recounted walking from one casino to another carrying a paper hat stuffed with $180,000 in cash. Amazingly, the MIT ring was never actually caught in the act. Some members retired. A few others were ratted out by a team traitor and banned from the casinos, which learned a lesson about the concept of team play.

BOWER BIRDS

USEFUL FOR: academic gatherings, impressing nerdy dates, and making small talk with art teachers

KEYWORDS: *This Old House*, *Trading Spaces*, or arts and crafts

THE FACT: While many male birds use elaborate visual signals to pique female interest, bower birds take more of a Bob Vila approach to the practice.

To attract a mate, these Australian birds carefully craft elaborate structures, called bowers. Amazingly, though, these structures turn out more like love mansions than love shacks. Using everything from leaves, sticks, and feathers to manmade items such as paper, cellophane and glass, these birds construct sturdy tunnels, towers, and archways. Some bowers include roofed bridges connecting two towers, while others have groomed lawns made from moss.

Once the bower is completed, the male calls out to females in the area, who, if impressed with the male's structure, will mate with him inside it. Interestingly, though, the bower only serves to show off the male's strength and vigor. After the mating is over, he tosses it aside along with the girl's phone number.

BOXING

*(and the guy you should **always** bet against)*

USEFUL FOR: consoling anyone who's ever lost a fight

KEYWORDS: jab, TKO, or I've seen grandmothers throw better punches

THE FACT: Despite being knocked out more than any professional boxer, the abysmal Bruce "the Mouse" Strauss isn't a sore loser.

In fact, Strauss proudly claims to have been knocked out on every continent except Antarctica. His career began in Oklahoma City in 1976 when the completely novice (and *drunk*) Strauss agreed to enter the ring as a last-minute replacement fighter for a match. Surprisingly, he won. Afterward, he became a professional boxer, though he never sought formal training. Later, he decided to fight as an "opponent," a boxer who almost exclusively fights inferior opponents in order to pad his or her record. By doing this, opponents can qualify for big fights to collect big checks, knowing with almost complete certainty that they won't win. This can lead to some pretty nasty losses, of which the Mouse had plenty. Of his strategy, Strauss once said, "If I couldn't knock 'em out, I'd look for a soft spot in the canvas, wait for a big punch, and close my eyes."

BRIDES

(the kind you could never afford)

USEFUL FOR: wedding rehearsal small talk, blowing a cheapskate's mind, scaring potential fathers of the bride, and consoling your parents after spending so much on your wedding dress

KEYWORDS: I do, for better or for worse, or doesn't this stuff ever go on sale

THE FACT: In possibly the most luxurious wedding in history, Vanisha Mittal, daughter of Anglo-Indian steel tycoon Lakshmi Mittal, married Amit Bhatia, an investment banker who literally cashed in.

The wedding, held in June 2004 in a chateau in France, lasted six days and was reported to have cost over $90 million (yes, that's U.S. dollars). The guest roster included some of Bollywood's brightest stars and some of Europe's deepest pockets. Among the expenditures: $520,000 for a performance by pop diva Kylie Minogue, who performed for a half hour. That's almost $300 per second, a figure even more shocking when you factor in dollars per unit of talent.

BUDDY RICH

(the original "Little Drummer Boy")

USEFUL FOR: barroom banter and anytime a country song plays on the jukebox

KEYWORDS: Buddy Rich, drumming, or child prodigy

THE FACT: Sure, Bernard "Buddy" Rich's technique and speed were impressive, but the fact that he never took a lesson and refused to practice outside of performances made him just plain unbelievable.

The son of vaudeville performers, Rich hit the stage in 1921 when he was only four years old and soon became the second-highest-paid child entertainer in the world. During his later career, he led some of the most successful big bands ever, and played with such greats as Tommy Dorsey, Dizzy Gillespie, and Louis Armstrong. But his drive and competitive nature also came with a volatile temper, which Rich was happy to showcase. He was notorious for screaming at his band members for hours on end (which they secretly tape-recorded) and fearlessly ridiculing pop stars during public interviews. Oh, and Rich also always needed to have the last word, even on his deathbed. While lying in a hospital after surgery, a nurse asked Rich if anything was bothering him. His response: "Yes . . . country music."

BURIALS

(where the early bird gets the body)

USEFUL FOR: when you're watching birds feed and making small talk at wakes

KEYWORDS: vultures, sky burials, or death

THE FACT: Many Parsis or Zoroastrians (who are mainly concentrated in Mumbai, India) have a truly unusual way of disposing of their dead . . . involving vultures.

They place corpses on a tower or on treetops to be devoured by vultures. It might seem crude at first, but it's religiously poetic. Because Parsis believe that nature is sacred, they choose not to defile the earth, fire, or water by using the elements to dispose of their bodies. Instead, they rely on vultures to perform a "sky burial" and leave little more than crumbs of bone to disintegrate. The practice is not wholly unique to the Parsis, though. Tibetan Buddhists in some areas of China perform comparable sky burials where the body of the deceased is first prepared, then distributed to dogs, crows, and vultures. Similarly, certain Bantu tribes in South Africa leave dead bodies for jackals to devour.

BUTTERED TOAST

USEFUL FOR: stunning your nerdy friends and definitively proving to your Charlie Brownish pals that they're just as unlucky as everyone else

KEYWORDS: my bread, dropped, or damn (usually in the form of "Damn! I dropped my bread")

THE FACT: The reports are in: Toast really does fall butterside down!

In an experiment led by physicist Robert Matthews of Aston University, British schoolchildren dropped thousands of buttered and unbuttered pieces of toast from their tables. The results are in: The buttered side will hit the ground first more often. In fact, irrespective of the buttering, the side of the toast facing up on the plate will probably hit the floor first. Why? Simply put, when the bread falls, it begins to flip. And it generally only has time to flip over once before it hits the floor, given the average kitchen table height—all of which leads to crying, whining, and restarting the whole toasting and buttering process. Oddly enough, in a related experiment, when the toast is dropped from a significantly higher height, the unbuttered side, on average, hits first.

THE CAN OPENER

(and the can)

USEFUL FOR: cocktail party banter, impressing history buffs, and sparking conversation anytime you see a tin of something

KEYWORDS: can, can opener, and which came first

THE FACT: While the *mental_floss* staff is still working around the clock to figure out that whole chicken/egg deal, the slightly less asked can opener/can question is definitely something we can answer.

In 1810, British merchant Peter Durand patented the tin can, allowing sterilized food to be preserved more effectively. The cans were useful for ocean voyages, during which glass bottles tended to break, and soon the British Navy was dining on canned veggies and meat. So far, so good. But what Durand (and everybody else for that matter) forgot to invent was a way to *open* the cans. For 50 years, getting into your pork 'n' beans required the use of a hammer and chisel. The can opener was patented by American inventor Ezra Warner in 1858, but even that wasn't particularly convenient. Early openers were stationed at groceries, and clerks did the honors. It wasn't until 1870 that the first home can openers made an appearance.

CASTRATION

(and Franz Joseph Haydn's pretty, pretty voice)

USEFUL FOR: chatting with choirmasters, piano teachers, and anyone who sings well

KEYWORDS: castration, sopranos, or castrated sopranos

THE FACT: As a kid, Haydn's voice was so beautiful that his choirmaster tried to trick him into keeping it forever via some delicate snipping.

Franz Joseph Haydn (1732-1809) was the father of the symphony as we know it. During more than 30 years of experimentation, he came up with the form that influences composers to this day. But as a little boy, Haydn was known for something else—his beautiful soprano voice. He was the star soprano in his church choir. As he got older and his voice was about to change, his choirmaster came to him with a little proposition. If he would consent to the small operation, he could keep his beautiful soprano voice forever. Haydn readily agreed, and was just about to undergo the surgery when his father found out and put a stop to the whole thing.

CHARLES II

(England's royal drain)

USEFUL FOR: impressing your history teacher, slackers, and any politician who isn't doing nearly enough

KEYWORDS: royalty, bum, or royal bums

THE FACT: Easily one of the most useless kings of all time, Charles II is on record as one of the laziest monarchs ever to "rule" Britain.

Some might argue that he played an important role just by showing up, because his restoration to the throne signaled a return to peace and tranquility after a bitter civil war. But once he got there Charles didn't do much of anything. A contemporary English chronicler, Samuel Pepys, described Charles as "A lazy Prince, no Council, no money, no reputation at home or abroad." Not the best PR. Even worse, a common saying at the time had it that Charles "never said a foolish thing, and never did a wise one." Ironically, the highpoint of Charles's popularity came when he survived an assassination attempt during the "Rye House Plot," named after the place where the would-be assassins allegedly wanted to kill him. After a lifetime spent not doing things, not getting killed was Charles's biggest accomplishment.

CHEESE ROLLING

USEFUL FOR: wine and cheese parties, chatting up extreme-sports enthusiasts or anyone from Wisconsin

KEYWORDS: cheese, England, or professional sports

THE FACT: Though it's without a doubt one of the most absurd sports on record, the annual cheese-rolling contest at Cooper's Hill in Gloucestershire, England, is also incredibly, incredibly dangerous.

Which isn't actually all that surprising when you consider how the sport is played. First, a master of ceremonies gives the countdown—"One to be ready, two to be steady, three to prepare, four to be off"—and then up to 20 contestants chase a 7-pound circular block of cheese down a steep, bumpy hillside, trying to catch it before it gets to the bottom, 300 yards below. Four games are played over the course of one day, including one for women. Video footage of past events shows contestants breaking bones and splitting heads open, with spectators suffering frequent injuries as contestants lose their footing and hurl themselves into the crowds. No one is quite sure how cheese rolling started, but it's great fun for those who have high thresholds (for watching) pain.

CHEMISTS

(specifically, the cockiest one we could find)

USEFUL FOR: book reports, science fairs, and chatting up scientists at science fairs

KEYWORDS: chemistry, modesty, or the periodic table

THE FACT: While Antoine-Laurent Lavoisier was the father of modern chemistry, he certainly wasn't the father of *modest* chemistry.

A buckshot Antoine once said, "I am young and avid for glory." His contributions no doubt precede him, including lighting the streets of Paris and establishing the law of conservation of mass. And though he often took too much credit for the ideas of others, his own contributions have lasted (he named oxygen and hydrogen—beat that!). Like all scientists, Lavoisier ran into some funding problems, so against the advice of his friends, he took a job as farmer-general (tax collector). That was his first mistake. His second was blackballing Jean-Paul Marat from the Academy of Sciences. During the French Revolution, the combination of Lavoisier's status as a tax collector for the government and Marat's influence landed Lavoisier at the guillotine. He supposedly begged for a few weeks to finish his experiments. Motion denied. Lavoisier was beheaded.

instant personalities

JACK KEROUAC skipped his high school graduation to sit in the sun and read Walt Whitman's *Leaves of Grass*.

Jazz legend **LOUIS ARMSTRONG** got his first Christmas tree at age 40, and liked it so much he took it on tour with him (for several months).

ALBERT EINSTEIN expressed little interest in improving his unruly appearance and was once mistaken for a staff electrician at a royal reception.

CHEWING GUM

USEFUL FOR: chatting with recent ex-smokers, four out of five dentists, and Violet "I Want It NOW" Beauregarde

KEYWORDS: Chiclets, Wrigley's, or Bazooka Joe

THE FACT: While you could thank Thomas Adams for that wad of mush you've been chewing now for 11 hours straight, you should also probably thank Santa Ana.

While Thomas Adams was the guy who turned what was essentially rubber into a mass-marketed foodstuff, he couldn't have done it without Texas villain Antonio Lopez de Santa Ana (yes, *that* Santa Ana). Exiled from Mexico in the late 1860s, Santa Ana moved to Staten Island, bringing with him some chicle, the gummy resin of the sapodilla tree. Chewing chicle was popular in Mexico, and Santa Ana introduced the pastime to some of his new American pals, including Thomas Adams. Adams wasn't the first to patent chewing gum, but he was the first to popularize it on a grand scale. Thanks to brilliant ideas such as the gumball, the gumball machine, and flavored gum, he successfully turned chicle into a multimillion-dollar business and, as some janitors would have you believe, the scourge of the earth.

CLAMS

(as in the very happiest ones around)

USEFUL FOR: cocktail parties, clam digs, and joking with psychiatrists

KEYWORDS: clams, Prozac, and other antidepressants

THE FACT: Everyone's heard the expression, but what happens when you try to squeeze a few extra smiles out of bivalves via some drugs?

Believe it or not, Gettysburg College researcher Peter Fong decided to dope up his subjects, fingernail clams, by putting them on antidepressants. And while the phrase "happy as a clam" didn't exactly originate with Fong's research, his unique Prozac prescription has kick-started their social lives. Prozac decreases the uptake of serotonin, making more of the neurosecretion available to the nervous system. In the bivalves' case, this led to an overwhelming urge for synchronous spawning—a boon both for clam farmers and gawky teenage clams alike.

CLICHÉS

(of a Nicaraguan sort)

USEFUL FOR: planning your itinerary, chatting up Latin Americans, and spotting a Nicaraguan Studies major from a fake

KEYWORDS: stereotypes, Nicaragua, or Mosquito Coast

THE FACT: If you're visiting Nicaragua and worried about having to brush up on all your high school Spanish, quit your worrying. Play your cards right and you can get by on English alone.

It's true. Just visit the Caribbean shore of Nicaragua—the idyllically named "Mosquito Coast"—and you'll find that English, Caribbean style, is the dominant tongue. And while it's a legacy of the days of British imperialism, the Nicaraguans are really fond of it. (Even Colombia has an English-speaking zone in the nearby islands of San Andres and Providencia.) In the 1980s, for example, the nation's leftist Sandinista rulers discovered to their chagrin just how deeply entrenched their country's cultural divide was. When they tried to root out English as the "language of imperialism," the people of the Caribbean coast quickly rose up in rebellion. We're guessing they only love the language that much because no one's ever forced them to diagram a sentence.

COCKROACHES

(and some serious animal magnetism)

USEFUL FOR: cocktail parties, impressing your biology teacher, perhaps even dating said biology teacher

KEYWORDS: too young, too old, too fat, or too bald

THE FACT: Not unlike some of the divorcées in your neighborhood, female cockroaches actually lower their dating standards when they start feeling old.

It's true. British scientists at the University of Manchester have determined that female cockroaches will lower their standards for a mate as their biological breeding clock begins to tick. By looking at the amount of wooing required of a cockroach male (similar to what's observed on college campuses worldwide), the researchers documented that females became less selective as their reproductive potential decreased. Males, however, seemed to show no difference in mating practices related to the female cockroach's age. Sound familiar?

COFFEE

USEFUL FOR: after-dinner conversation, impressing lit majors, chatting up anyone who really loves their Joe

KEYWORDS: Starbucks, Maxwell House, Taster's Choice, etc.

THE FACT: No matter how much you need your morning jolt of caffeine, Balzac needed his more.

"Coffee is a great power in my life," the French writer said in his essay "The Pleasures and Pains of Coffee." "I have observed its effects on an epic scale." The thing is, he wasn't kidding. Balzac consumed as many as 50 cups of strong Turkish coffee per day, and we're talking about the days before indoor plumbing! Of course, he was no slouch at eating, either. At one meal old Balzac was reported to have eaten 100 oysters, 12 mutton cutlets, a duck, two partridges, and some fish, along with desserts, fruits, and wine. But coffee was clearly his passion, and he was faithful to the end. When Balzac couldn't get it strong enough, the addict was known to down pulverized coffee beans to get the kick he needed. This produced two results: Balzac was an incredibly energetic and prolific writer, writing more than 100 novels. He also died of caffeine poisoning at the age of 51.

CONDIMENTS

(Eskimo style)

USEFUL FOR: when you're out of ketchup and no one wants to run to the store

KEYWORDS: seal, oil, or do you want any sauce with that?

THE FACT: Forget ketchup and salsa, Inuits (often called "Eskimos") consider raw seal oil the king of all condiments.

In fact, the Inuits are quite happy to slather the excellent sauce on baked salmon, sheefish, whitefish, caribou, moose, and anything else you can catch up north. Inuits also like their seal oil on "frozen-raw" moose or caribou and fish. So what's the secret to this not-so-secret sauce? The oil is produced by cutting up freshly slaughtered seal blubber into chunks and leaving them outside in a bucket for five days, stirring occasionally, until the blubber naturally renders and becomes oil. An adult seal produces about 5 gallons of usable seal oil. Once ready, just add A-1 or Tabasco to taste (really)!

CONDUCTORS

(as in the first guy to die wielding a baton)

USEFUL FOR: cocktail parties, classical performances, and just in case you ever happen to be stuck in an elevator with Zubin Mehta

KEYWORDS: orchestra, conductors, or "the Meistro"

THE FACT: Believe it or not, the very first orchestra conductor died in the act (of conducting).

Jean-Baptiste Lully (1632–1687) was the first documented conductor. Before him, most musical groups followed their first violinist or their keyboard player. Lully was the first musician ever to use a baton. However, his "baton" was a heavy staff, six feet long, which he pounded on the ground in time to the music. Unfortunately, this staff proved to be his undoing. One day, while merrily beating time (in a concert to celebrate Louis XIV's return to health), he stuck the staff into his foot by mistake. He developed gangrene and died. Not a good role model for conductors worldwide.

CROSSED EYES

(and the philosopher who loved 'em)

USEFUL FOR: cocktail parties, academic gatherings, convincing your pal there's *probably* someone out there that'll find 'em attractive (don't make any promises)

KEYWORDS: free will, philosophy, Descartes, or really bizarre fantasy

THE FACT: Father of Modern Philosophy and smooth operator René "I Think Therefore I Am" Descartes liked his women cross-eyed.

It's true. Apparently, old René had a thing for cross-eyed women thanks to a childhood fascination with a cross-eyed playmate. And as if the fact weren't strange enough, the case might be the only example of a sexual fetish changing the history of Western thought. As he describes in the *Principles of Philosophy*, after working hard at it for a while Descartes was finally able to condition his body to find straight-eyed women attractive (good for Descartes, maybe, but a disaster for the hard-up, cross-eyed ladies of Europe). But it was actually this experience that led him to believe in free will and helped him come to the conclusion that the mind can control the body's impulses.

CRUISE CONTROL

(and the blind guy who invented it)

USEFUL FOR: cocktail parties, dates, chatting up engineers, and actually impressing just about anyone

KEYWORDS: Helen Keller, speeding tickets, or motion sickness

THE FACT: You know that gadget that keeps your lead foot from giving you a ticket? Well, it was invented by a blind guy.

Seriously! His name's Ralph Teetor, and he was blinded in a shop accident at age five, but apparently harbored no resentment for sharp tools. In fact, he went on to attend college and became one of the most respected mechanical engineers of his era. While Teetor was responsible for a lot of vehicular improvements, including automatic transmission, he's best known for making it possible for even leadfoots to stick to one speed. Apparently, inspiration struck during World War II, when the government set a 35 mph speed limit to conserve gas and tires. The inventor came up with a device that could regulate car speed without the driver touching the gas pedal. After a few tweaks and many dubious names (including "controlomatic" and "speedostat"), cruise control premiered in select 1958 Chrysler models. It soon became an $86 option known as "autopilot."

CRUSADES

(how to wipe your sin slate clean)

USEFUL FOR: stirring up philosophical discussion, impressing academics, and chatting up anyone trying to incite religious wars (not that you should know such people)

KEYWORDS: holy war, holy crusade, or holy crap

THE FACT: By the 11th century, the Christian Church was split into eastern and western factions, and the holy city of Jerusalem had been under control of the Muslims for a couple hundred years. That is, until Pope Urban II had a big idea.

In 1095, Pope Urban II summoned clergy and nobles to a council in the village of Clermont in central France. After listing a number of alleged atrocities on eastern Christians by the Muslims and arguing the need to recapture Jerusalem, the pope cajoled the crowd into taking up arms against the so-called heathens. And with a flair for the dramatic, the pope stated that "God wills it." Of course, Urban did come up with a clever scheme for paying the warriors. For going to the Holy Land and fighting the Muslims, crusaders were offered a heck of a deal: Not only would their past sins be forgiven, but present and future ones as well! With free passes to heaven on the horizon, armies of crusaders stormed toward the Holy Land, changing the region forever.

D-DAY

(or nap time for Hitler in Germany)

USEFUL FOR: impressing history buffs, irritating fans of afternoon slumber, and spurring discussions on the demise of Nazi Germany

KEYWORDS: World War II, drowsy, or nap time

THE FACT: The weather seemed too rough over the English Channel the evening of June 5, 1944, to launch the greatest military invasion in history. So Adolf Hitler figured "What the heck, I'm going to bed."

Der Führer took a sleeping pill and left orders not to be disturbed. Big mistake on old Adolf's part: D-day was several hours into effect before aides got the courage to wake Hitler up to get his permission to mobilize needed troops and equipment. Even then, the dictator dallied. He had tea, took a nap, and met with the premier of Hungary. Finally, about 5 P.M. on June 6, he issued orders, mostly bad ones, that kept German generals from being able to move reinforcements to the invasion area. Good thing for the Allies that he woke up.

DALI

(and his surrealist tricks)

USEFUL FOR: cocktail parties, chatting up struggling artists, and anyone carrying a pan and a spoon

KEYWORDS: Dali, surrealism, or napping

THE FACT: Who knew Dali's greatest creative moments were inspired by a little interrupted sleep?

Salvador Dali, the Spanish surrealist painter, arrived at the startling images of his most productive period—between 1929 and 1937—using what he called the "paranoiac-critical method." Apparently, this involved fishing "delirious associations and interpretations" out of his unconscious. It's less than clear how he accomplished this, but he used no intoxicants. "I don't do drugs," he once said. "I am drugs." Dali wasn't above manipulating his consciousness in other ways, though. He reportedly took odd little cat naps that brought him right to the edge of deep sleep, but then jerked himself out of it. His method was simple: Seated in an armchair, Dali held a metal spoon in one hand. Then next to his chair, he placed a metal pan. He'd quickly nod off, and as soon as he was relaxed enough to let go of the spoon, it would fall against the pan. The sudden clang waking him up, Dali was immediately reacquainted with his subconscious and went back to work.

DEADBEAT DAD

(and a repeat offender at that)

USEFUL FOR: cocktail parties, barroom banter, chatting up anyone from a big family

KEYWORDS: fertility, virility, or Viagra

THE FACT: How many Polish kings does it take to father an estimated 365 illegitimate children? Just one.

That king is Frederick Augustus of Saxony, better known as August II ("the Strong"), King of Poland (1670–1733). Famous as a man of immense physical strength, unquenchable lust, and, apparently, considerable stamina, they didn't call old August "strong" for nothin'. The first of his 300-plus love children was Hermann Maurice, Comte de Saxe, a military genius who himself had several illegitimate children. The great female French novelist George Sand is descended from both these men. However, with that many children between them, we probably all are.

TCHAIKOVSKY suffered from a paralyzing fear that his head would fall off his body, and often conducted orchestras with one hand holding his head.

A romantic to the end, the famous T'ang dynasty poet **LI PO** died when, in a drunken state, he tried to embrace the reflection of the moon in a lake and fell in.

It was often joked that comedian **LOU COSTELLO**'s house was furnished in "early Universal" as in Universal Studios, because the slightly klepto Costello had a habit of taking home (and keeping) so many props during filming.

DEATH

(by green potato chips)

USEFUL FOR: any gathering where there's a plateful of chips and a couple of people with working ears

KEYWORDS: heart attack, poison, or party by the chip bowl

THE FACT: We've all seen the occasional stray green potato chip lingering strangely among their crispy golden friends. The question is: Will chowing down on a few really kill you?

Luckily, eating a green potato chip won't do you harm—eating a ton of those suckers, though, definitely will. Green chips generally come from a potato that grew partially above the ground, where the sunlight makes it produce chlorophyll. These potatoes also create a substance called solanine that is, in fact, toxic and can cause problems. The good news is that you'd have to eat several pounds of the stuff at once to notice any major effect, and if you're chomping down that many taters, you'll probably die of a heart attack long before the toxins set in.

DIABETES

(and a poodle's piddle)

USEFUL FOR: chatting with scientists, breaking the silence after your dog goes on someone else's lawn, carpet, or doormat

KEYWORDS: I can't believe your dog just went on my lawn, carpet, or doormat

THE FACT: Who could have known that a puddle of dog urine would spur the treatment for diabetes?

That's right! In studying the function of the pancreas (which wasn't well understood in 1889), two professors from the University of Strassburg decided to remove the pancreas from a living dog. Later, flies were seen swarming around the canine's urine. Curious as to the cause, the professors analyzed the sample and found that it contained a higher-than-normal amount of sugar. The doggone discovery led the scientists to determine a relationship between the pancreas and its control of insulin. In turn, this led to the first effective treatment of diabetes through insulin injections.

DICTATORS

(a really, really fat one)

USEFUL FOR: impressing 4th-grade teachers, nerdy dates, bullies with weight problems (hey, someone's gotta give 'em hope!)

KEYWORDS: hefty, healthy, pudgy, paunchy, big boned, or obese

THE FACT: The crown for the world's chubbiest autocrat goes to the longtime king of Tonga, Taufa'ahau Tupou IV, weighing in at a lovable 462 pounds.

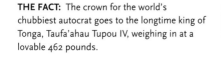

Nothing establishes power over the people quite like making it abundantly obvious to them that you have access to more food than they do. Just think of the adorably pudgy (and slightly paranoid) Kim Jong Il or the rotund Idi Amin. But by far the fattest autocrat is Taufa'ahau Tupou IV of Tonga. But don't let the chub fool you: despite weighing in at a clunky 400-plus pounds, the Tongan king is 100 percent dictator. And, in fact, he can be pretty unpleasantly plump. For instance, he actually led one of the strangest imperialist campaigns of all time. After an eccentric Nevadan named Michael Oliver piled sand onto a reef in the Pacific and declared his newly built paradise the Republic of Minerva in 1972, Tupou and a force of 350 Tongans invaded the one-man nation and annexed it in history's most minor act of colonialism.

DINOSAURS

(specifically, one that never existed)

USEFUL FOR: impressing preschool teachers, preschool students, and anyone fond of the gentle giant Brontosaurus

KEYWORDS: *Jurassic Park*, *The Land Before Time*, or anytime you spot a dinosaur Band-Aid

THE FACT: No matter what you remember from school, the Brontosaurus never existed. Apparently, someone's been making a fool out of you for far too long.

Turns out there's no such thing. In 1874, scientist O. C. Marsh uncovered dinosaur fossils in Wyoming and thought he'd discovered another prehistoric genus, which he named *Brontosaurus*. What Marsh didn't find was the body's head, but that didn't stop him from constructing a full-scale model of the "newly discovered" dinosaur. He just used the head of a Camarasaurus, even though it was a drastically different genus. When scientists finally found out about the great head switcheroo in the early 1970s, they revealed the Brontosaurus for what it really was: an Apatosaurus with a Camarasaurus head. In 1974, the name was formally rejected, but many elementary school teachers still haven't gotten the memo.

DISPENSERS

(of the PEZ variety)

USEFUL FOR: chatting with kids and ex-smokers, and making pals with those with a sweet tooth

KEYWORD: PEZ

THE FACT: The first PEZ dispensers were actually made for adults, and made to look like lighters to help nonsmokers fit in.

The whole PEZ craze started back in 1927 when Austrian baker and candy maker J. Eduard Haas and a chemist friend developed the first cold-pressed hard candies. Mint flavored and wrapped in paper, these originals bore little resemblance to today's PEZ other than the name, derived from PfeffErminZ, the German word for "peppermints." Like we said, PEZ wasn't even a children's candy. Haas marketed his creation to adults, hyping it as a way to stop smoking—like nicotine gum, but without the rush. In fact, when Haas made the first PEZ dispensers almost two decades later, he designed them to look and work like Zippo lighters. When everyone else was lighting up, PEZ users could flick their own "lighter" and pop a peppermint instead. The brand's familiar plastic heads didn't appear until 1950, after PEZ arrived in North America and shed its medicinal image for those of cult heroes like Popeye and Santa Claus.

DIVINITY SCHOOL

(and a dropout with a really bad rep)

USEFUL FOR: cocktail parties, first dates, and Sunday school

KEYWORDS: Casanova, Catholicism, quitters, or sex

THE FACT: Giacomo ("Jacques") Casanova, as in the 18th century's most notorious cad, actually began his lecherous escapades as a seminary student.

That is, until he was expelled under "cloudy circumstances" (we're guessing it was for sleeping with someone). As you well know, everyone's favorite 18th-century libertine led a postseminary life that's as ungodly as it gets. By the age of 30 he was sentenced to prison for engaging in "magic," but he escaped after only a year to Paris. Oddly enough, he made a fortune there by introducing the lottery to France. But before settling down to pen his ribald, self-aggrandizing autobiography, Casanova was expelled from more European countries than most of us will ever get to visit. Along the way, he slept with tons of women, dueled with many of their husbands, and generally sinned his way to the top of European culture, befriending such figures as Madame de Pompadour and Jean-Jacques Rousseau along the way.

DIXIE CUPS

USEFUL FOR: chatting at watercoolers and whenever you find yourself using a Dixie Cup, really

KEYWORDS: Dixie, Harvard, or Kansas's greatest contribution to drinking

THE FACT: Who knew it was a Harvard dropout who started the little cup craze that swept the nation?

You can thank Hugh Moore, Dixie Cup genius, and Ivy League underachiever for putting his education, or lack thereof, to good use. It all started in 1909, when Kansas's Board of Health outlawed public wells and communal water dippers based on the novel logic that they spread disease. Unfortunately, this left Kansans at a loss for a way to distribute water. Enter Moore. He invented an ice-chilled dispenser that served customers five ounces of water in a disposable paper cup. Moore's Health Kups didn't exactly take the country by storm, but they sold well enough to keep him in business until 1919, when he thought of a better name. The choice was Dixie. Moore adopted the name from the Dixie Doll Company in New York, simply because he liked the sound of the word. And judging from the increase in post–name-change sales, so did most of America.

DOUBLE DECAF

(of the Jell-O variety)

USEFUL FOR: after-dinner conversation, making small talk at Starbucks, and anytime you see a Jell-O mold

KEYWORDS: grande, jiggle, or Pudding Pops

THE FACT: Just one of the many odd flavors they experimented with, in 1918, the makers of Jell-O introduced a new flavor: coffee. No one went wild for it.

Its release was ostensibly based on the logic that, since lots of people like to drink coffee with dessert, they'd be game for combining the two after-dinner treats. Not the case. The company soon realized if anyone wants dessert coffee, they're going to have a cup of it. In fact, if anyone wants coffee *at all,* they're going to have a cup of it. Not surprisingly, this realization came at about the time they yanked the product off the shelves. All in all, it hasn't harmed the company too much. At least they learned their lesson, right? Wrong. Cola-flavored Jell-O was sold for about a year starting in 1942, and for a brief while the wiggly dessert was sold in celery and apple flavors, too.

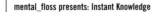

DOWNSIZING

(in the ancient Icelandic form)

USEFUL FOR: barroom banter, chatting with Vikings fans (more the historical than the football kind)

KEYWORDS: insults, Iceland, downsizing, or punishment

THE FACT: What's a poor farmer to do when his honor is insulted by three servants of a wealthy landowner? According to ancient Icelandic sagas, if you're Thorstein Thorarinsson, you kill 'em.

Of course, then you've got to announce your actions after the fact in accordance with ancient Icelandic custom. Luckily for Thorstein, the three he killed were so worthless that their own boss didn't particularly want to avenge them. Thorstein and the chieftain, a chap named Bjarni, fought a rather half-hearted duel, punctuated by frequent water breaks, pauses to examine one another's weapons, and even stops to tie their shoes in mid-battle. Finally, they reached a settlement: Thorstein, who was strong enough to do the work of three men, became the perfect replacement for the three he had killed. Downsizing, Icelandic style.

ELEPHANTS

(gone wild)

USEFUL FOR: circus dates, safaris, discussions on single (elephant) parenting

KEYWORDS: elephant, rage, teenage rebellion

THE FACT: In 1995, rangers at South Africa's Pilanesberg National Park began finding dead rhinos, brutally battered and mutilated. An investigation was launched, and it led them to a surprising realization: the raucous culprits were teenage elephants.

Many of the thuggish elephants were turning increasingly violent, and had added rhino murder to their rap sheets. But why all the charges? Apparently, the young bulls were entering a period known as *musth*, or heightened aggression related to mating, at a younger age and for longer periods than normal for teens. Wildlife biologists also realized that the youngsters in the park—populated by relocated animals—lacked the structure they needed. When a few older, and perhaps wiser, bulls were added to the park, it forced the young'uns to return to their place in the elephant hierarchy. But not only did the adult supervision give them a bit of social order; it actually repressed the teens' testosterone levels, delaying and shortening musth. The elephant-on-rhino crimes stopped soon after.

THE ELITIST DICTIONARY

USEFUL FOR: academic gatherings, making friends at Mensa, and amusing anyone who finds fault with good old Webster's

KEYWORDS: pretentious, pompous, or arrogant

THE FACT: Fed up with reading one boring dictionary after the other (who isn't!), lexicographer Eugene Ehrlich decided to publish *The Highly Selective Dictionary for the Extraordinarily Literate*. Clearly, the act of a modest man.

Reportedly uninterested in contributing to the "forces of linguistic darkness," this freedom fighter of pretentiousness dedicates his pages to concentrating on unusual words that normal dictionaries may not take the time to fully explain. His companion to the book, *The Highly Selective Thesaurus for the Extraordinarily Literate*, provides synonyms to the kinds of fancy words he covers in his dictionary, inadvertently offering the "extraordinarily literate" a list of words they probably learned in elementary school.

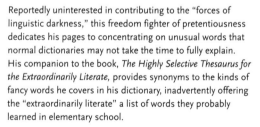

END OF THE WORLD

(almost)

USEFUL FOR: putting some real fear into people who like *Fear Factor*, scaring anyone, and making a room go silent

KEYWORDS: Suez Crisis, nuclear holocaust, or "look at those beautiful swans"

THE FACT: On November 5, 1956, during the Suez Crisis, the North American Aerospace Defense Command (NORAD) received warnings that indicated a large-scale Soviet attack was under way. Read wrong, it could have started a third world war.

Signs showed that a Soviet fleet was moving from the Black Sea to a more aggressive posture in the Aegean, 100 Soviet MiGs were flying over Syria, a British bomber had been shot down in Syria, and unidentified aircraft were in flight over Turkey, causing the Turkish air force to go on high alert. All signs pointed to the ominous, except that each of the four warnings was found to have a completely innocent explanation. The Soviet fleet was conducting routine exercises, the MiGs were part of an escort for the president of Syria, the British bomber had made an emergency landing after mechanical problems, and, last but not least, the unidentified planes over Turkey turned out to be a large flock of swans.

ESCALATORS

(fun for the feeble-minded)

USEFUL FOR: cocktail parties, amusement park lines, definitively convincing any kid that things were a lot more boring before their time

KEYWORDS: Who knows how the first escalator came about?

THE FACT: The original escalator wasn't so much a moving staircase as a really big ramp.

In 1891, Jesse Reno patented the first escalator, paving the way for today's world—one in which we choose not to use staircases, just StairMasters! But Reno's initial invention was more of an inclined ramp than the escalator we know today, where passengers hooked into cleats on the belt and scooted up at a 25-degree angle. Fairly soon after, he built a spiral escalator—the mere thought of which nauseates us—in London, but it was never used by the public. Reno's first escalator, though, was *widely* used, albeit not practically. In a testament to how utterly unamusing amusement parks were in the 1890s, 75,000 people rode Reno's "inclined elevator" during a two-week exhibition at Coney Island in 1896. Let's be clear: The escalator was not the means by which one traveled to a ride. It was the ride itself.

JESSE JAMES, the lawless, murderin' bank robber, went by the nickname "Dingus" in honor of the time he accidentally shot off the tip of his finger. Without so much as wincing, James looked down and said, "Ain't that the most dingus-dangest thing you ever seen?"

Italian violinist **NICCOLÒ PAGANINI** used to saw partway through the strings on his violin so that during a show three would break. In fact, his one-string performance led to widespread rumors that he'd sold his soul to the devil.

Apparently, the real portrait of the artist is that of a confused man: Writer **JAMES JOYCE** liked wearing five wristwatches on his arm, each set to a different time.

EVA PERÓN

USEFUL FOR: making snide comments whenever someone forces you to watch *Evita*

KEYWORDS: Madonna, dictators' wives, or "Don't Cry for Me, Argentina"

THE FACT: While Ms. Perón definitely has a bit of a sob story and a rags-to-riches tale, you really shouldn't feel obligated to cry for her.

"Saint Evita" was the daughter of an adulterous relationship between two villagers in an impoverished part of Argentina. She made a name for herself as an actress before marrying Juan Perón in 1944, but, being illegitimate (and a peasant), she was never really accepted in the social circles in which he routinely traveled. As a rising military officer, Perón quickly found himself dictator of Argentina, and "Evita" was by his side. In fact, she was more than just there to wave at crowds and manage the mansion. Evita actually ran several government ministries and almost became vice president in 1951 (the military bullied Perón into making her drop out of the campaign). And though she's best known in the United States from the musical and movie that bear her name, the flick plays up the glamour and romance of her career while largely ignoring her corruption, oppression of political rivals, cozying up to Nazi war criminals, and other questionable doings.

EXECUTION

(and a lopping mistake)

USEFUL FOR: impressing history buffs, making small talk on death row

KEYWORDS: guillotine, execution, or flat-out wrong

THE FACT: Despite what you may think, Dr. Joseph-Ignace Guillotin did *not* invent the guillotine, though the contraption is named for him.

The doctor's name was Guillotin, with no final *e,* and he was deputy to the French States-General in 1789. A supporter of capital punishment, he thought it should be done uniformly, with merciful efficiency, and proposed a head-chopping device. Of course, such machines had been around for centuries. After the States-General became the revolutionary General Assembly, French *Procureur General Syndic* Pierre-Louis Roederer turned not to Guillotin, but another doctor, Antoine Louis, for a design. And, in fact, it was a German engineer who built the first working model. While it's not clear how the machine came to be named for Guillotin, we do know why it's spelled that way. The final *e* was added to make it easier to rhyme with in revolutionary ballads.

EX-LAX

USEFUL FOR: any situation where you feel comfortable enough, really

KEYWORDS: bathroom, prunes, or great Hungarians

THE FACT: While Max Kiss told everyone that the name he picked for the medication he invented, Ex-Lax, stood for "excellent laxative," the word originally came from a slang term he found in a Hungarian newspaper referring to parliamentary deadlock.

Definitely strange but true. As for the product itself, in 1905, the Hungarian immigrant and pharmacist, Kiss, went on vacation in the old country, and while en route aboard ship, a physician told him about a new tasteless powder laxative produced by Bayer. It was one small step for the drug company, but one giant leap for humanity, which had been previously plagued by foul-tasting, not-altogether-gentle laxatives such as castor oil and tea made from moss. Kiss set off on a series of flavor experiments that eventually led to the chocolate-flavored medication still sold today. Oddly enough, though, Ex-Lax did try to expand its taste roster, but with dubious results. Early in the company's history, Kiss tried to turn the American public on to a *fig-flavored* drink version, but it went over like a lead balloon.

FAN CLUBS

(a.k.a. A Groupie Kind of Love)

USEFUL FOR: cocktail parties, making friends at obedience school, and lamenting with all the other rock stars how hard having an enormous fan base is

KEYWORDS: dog, Beatlemania, Liszt, or haircuts

THE FACT: Believe it or not, the Beatles weren't the first stars to have such an insane following. In fact, Franz Liszt was a rock star before rock was invented. And he even had to buy a dog to cope with the fame (but not for the reasons you'd think).

There's a reason musicians only give out autographs these days. The Hungarian Franz Liszt (1811–1886), a virtuoso in the tradition of Paganini, played the piano and created a sensation throughout Europe. Everywhere he toured, women swooned—and he sometimes swooned himself. Liszt was one of the first rock stars, and the word *Lisztomania* was actually coined during his lifetime. In fact, he used to receive so many requests for a lock of his hair that he finally bought a dog, snipping off patches of fur to send to his admirers. An unexpected use for your best friend.

FISHING

(for answers)

USEFUL FOR: chatting up nerds and scientists, and making small talk at bait shops

KEYWORD: Teflon

THE FACT: If it weren't for a fortuitous fishing trip and a curious Frenchman, the wonders of Teflon might never have seen light of day.

Roy Plunkett discovered Teflon (tetrafluoroethylene) in a Du Pont lab in 1938 during the search for a new refrigerant. Much like Spencer Silver's Post-it notes, though, it was tossed aside for lack of application. In fact, it wasn't even considered for commercial production until a Frenchman named Marc Gregoire went fishing. Gregoire found that the substance worked great on his tackle to reduce tangling. Of course, now Teflon is used in everything from car brakes to space suits to replacement arteries for the human heart. It's also used on microchips, rockets, and, surprisingly, it's even rubbed liberally on the Statue of Liberty's arthritic joints (Teflon apparently slows down the aging process in statues).

THE FLASHLIGHT

USEFUL FOR: chatting up inventors, nerdy dates, and anytime you lose electricity

KEYWORDS: flashlight, flashbulb, or two "C" batteries

THE FACT: If you're looking for a reason to break out the good stationery, why don't you send a note to Russian novelty-shop owner Akiba Horowitz, inventor of the flashlight.

It all started in 1896, when Horowitz (also known as Conrad Hubert, his postimmigration name) bought the rights to a funny little gag gift called the electric flowerpot. As the name implies, the gadget consisted of a battery and a light bulb that sat inside a pot and lit up a fake flower. Horowitz remarketed the thing as a bicycle lamp, but the product was less than successful. Then Mr. H joined forces with David Misel, an inventor who had designed an early tubular lighting device. Apparently, it was a match made in lighting heaven. Horowitz took the improved version of the pot to the people, now selling it as a battery-operated candle replacement. The rest is history. As for the moniker, however, the "flashlight" picked up the name because the limitations of contemporary batteries meant you had to continuously switch the light on and off.

FLIRTING

(Victorian style)

USEFUL FOR: talking about how lame the Victorians were

KEYWORDS: hand fans, come-ons, or secret codes

THE FACT: In the Victorian age, an eligible Victor couldn't just cruise up to a Victoria and put the moves on her. No, in the extraordinarily prudish age proper etiquette had to be maintained at all times.

However, that didn't exactly mean that flirting was off-limits at social events. In fact, it was pretty en vogue. And one of the most subtle ways of demonstrating interest or disinterest was with the use of hand fans. In fact, a whole sign language was created around fan movements and placement. If a young lady let her fan rest on her right cheek it meant she was interested, if she placed it on the left, however, it meant the guy was being passed over (subtle, but harsh!). Similarly, if she moved the fan slowly it was a signal that she was already engaged or married. If she held the fan in front of her face with her right hand it was a signal for the young man to follow her. Finally, if she moved the fan across her forehead it meant they were being watched. Whew! With all the mixed signals, restrictions, and rites of courtship, it's a wonder anyone found time to procreate.

FORESKINS

(and the best darn moyel in the Bible)

USEFUL FOR: weddings, circumcisions, anytime you want to say the words *Bible* and *foreskin* in the same sentence

KEYWORDS: David, Goliath, or dowry

THE FACT: If you know where to look, you can find all kinds of crazy stuff in the Good Book, including tales of insane dowries and circumcisions.

It's true! So grab your King James Version and flip to chapter 18 of the first book of Samuel for the story of David (yes, *that* David, with the stone and the sling and the psalms) and Michal. After David smote the heck out of Philistine badass Goliath, he went to live with King Saul of Israel. Saul, afraid of David and troubled by evil spirits, began to plot his murder. When Saul's daughter Michal revealed her love for David, Saul made her a deal: Have David bring back 100 Philistine foreskins, and he can marry you. Now Saul had no particular affinity for foreskins; he just wanted David to get killed trying. But Dave and his posse, with God's help, brought back 200 for the good king. Saul couldn't help but bless his daughter's marriage to such a go-getter.

FORGERIES

(only the best darn ones in the whole wide world)

USEFUL FOR: cocktail parties, museum dates, and making someone double-guess themselves after buying "authentic" artwork

KEYWORDS: real, genuine, and one of a kind

THE FACT: What made Elmyr de Hory infamous wasn't the sheer number of forgeries he sold. It was that they were damn *good* forgeries.

For 30 years, de Hory sold forgeries of paintings by the world's greatest artists, including Picasso, Chagall, Matisse, Degas, and Toulouse-Lautrec. In fact, his forgeries were so good, so precise in every detail, that they fooled even the most experienced art buyers—so much so that the native Hungarian has even attracted a cult following of his own, who pay high prices for "authentic" de Hory fakes. Irony of ironies, the forger's forgeries are now being forged and sold by other forgers! Even more odd, today legitimate museums host exhibitions of de Hory's works. De Hory told his story in the 1969 biography, *Fake!* by Clifford Irving (who went on to, yes, forge an autobiography of Howard Hughes). But in the end the master forger wound up penniless (just like a real painter) and committed suicide in 1976, although rumors persist that he faked that, too.

FORMAL WEAR

(according to Einstein)

USEFUL FOR: cocktail parties, fashion shows, and justifying your dressed-down appearance anywhere

KEYWORDS: the invitation did say black tie

THE FACT: Albert Einstein wasn't exactly the snazziest dresser of them all. But who knew he hated getting gussied up so much?

Sure, you know all about Uncle Albert's famous equations, his knack for the violin, his love of sailing, or maybe even that he was offered the presidency of the newly created Israel in 1948. But did you know that he was a notoriously bad dresser? That's right, unkempt hair and all, Albert Einstein was a poster boy for unruly appearances. In fact, he was so underdressed on one occasion (a reception with the emperor of the Austro-Hungarian empire no less) that he was mistaken for an electrician because of his work shirt. Not surprisingly, Albert also disliked extravagance, claiming that luxuries were wasted on him. Despite his intellectual celebrity status, the Nobel Prize winner refused to travel in anything but third class.

FREEMASONS

USEFUL FOR: Mummers parades, Shriners conventions, and whenever you spot a bizarre handshake

KEYWORDS: The Craft, the Grand Geometrician, or Colonel Sanders

THE FACT: The granddaddy of all not-so-secret secret societies, Freemasonry, or "The Craft," as its members call it, actually has its roots in medieval stoneworkers' guilds.

Mason lore, however, extends its origins back to biblical times, linking the society to the building of the Temple of Solomon. One thing's for sure, though, freemasonry is split into numerous subgroups and orders, and all of them consider God the Grand Geometrician, or Grand Architect of the Universe. At their hearts, these groups are all means of exploring ethical and philosophical issues, and are famous (or infamous) for their rituals and symbols. Take, for instance, the use of secret handshakes and passwords, all collectively known as the modes of recognition. Not surprisingly, the list of famous masons is massive, explaining the many conspiracy theories regarding the Masons' influence and intentions. Mozart, FDR, George Washington, Mark Twain, Voltaire, Benjamin Franklin, John Wayne, Jesse Jackson, and Colonel Sanders were all Masons.

FUNERAL FEASTS

(that are sinfully delicious)

USEFUL FOR: making small talk at morgues, wakes, and anytime you get a hankering for some evil

KEYWORDS: sin, confession, or cake

THE FACT: If you're looking for a meal that's sinfully delicious, you might want to head to Wales, where the ancient custom of "sin-eating" still takes place.

According to the practice, foods are waved over a loved one's body so that they will "absorb" the deceased's sins. Afterward, mourners chow down on the grub as a way of consuming any mischief done, ensuring that the body's spirit can pass on to the next world squeaky-clean. On the other end of the spectrum, however, if you're looking to pick up some new talents (like enough rhythm to dance in public), Bavaria might be your funeral destination of choice. According to ancient custom, unleavened cakes (later to be baked) are placed on a corpse. The sweets are supposed to soak up the loved one's virtues, and distribute them to anyone feasting on the dessert.

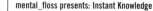

GANDHI

(the most Nobel loser of them all)

USEFUL FOR: impressing your history teacher or nerdy dates, or consoling anyone who wanted more than just the honor of being nominated

KEYWORDS: Gandhi, Nobel Peace Prize, screwed

THE FACT: The Susan Lucci of Nobel Peace Prize contenders, Mohandas "Mahatma" (Great Soul) Gandhi was nominated like crazy: 1937, 1938, 1939, 1947, and 1948, but never actually won!

Most people would agree that Gandhi certainly deserved the Peace Prize. After all, his name is basically synonymous with peace. Even more convincing, though, is the fact that his nonviolent methods helped kick the British out of India and became the model for future Peace laureates like Martin Luther King Jr. Actually, when Gandhi's final nomination came in 1948, he was the odds-on favorite to win that year. However, the "Mahatma" was assassinated just a few days before the deadline. Since a Nobel Prize is never awarded posthumously, the prize for Peace went unawarded that year on the grounds that there was "no suitable living candidate." The decision was also motivated by the fact that Gandhi left no heirs or foundations to which his prize money could go.

GENGHIS KHAN

(and a good reason not to mourn him)

USEFUL FOR: wakes, or impressing history professors, camel lovers, and Indiana Jones

KEYWORDS: Genghis Khan, buried treasure, or dromedaries

THE FACT: On August 18, 1227, Genghis Khan, the most feared leader of the 13th century, was buried along with a simple procession of 2,500 followers and a mounted bodyguard of 400 soldiers. Of course, no one lived to tell about it except a camel.

It's true. Anyone unfortunate enough to happen upon the procession was immediately put to death by the soldiers. Upon arriving at a remote mountain location in Mongolia, 40 virgins were killed to provide Khan with the needed pleasures in the afterlife. Then, at the end of the funeral ceremony, the soldiers killed all 2,500 members of the procession. When the 400 soldiers returned to Khan's capital city, *they* were immediately put to death by another group of soldiers so that no one could reveal where Khan's final resting place was. So did anyone survive the onslaught? Well, yes—a camel. The creature was spared since she could find her way back to the site if Khan's family wanted to visit.

GERMOPHOBES

(one cokehead, to be exact)

USEFUL FOR: cocktail parties, impressing history teachers, and chatting up interior designers

KEYWORDS: cocaine, bathrooms, or OCD

THE FACT: Picture every stereotypical South American drug dealer you've ever seen in a movie. They're all based in part on Pablo Emilio Escobar Gaviria, except for the obsessive-compulsive part.

As the head of the Colombian Medellin drug cartel, Escobar ran his ruthless empire from a lavish pad complete with Arabian horses, a miniature bullfighting ring, a private landing strip, and a private army of bodyguards. Clearly, money wasn't an object for the man. After all, he could afford to pay local authorities $250,000 each to turn a blind eye. Plus, he used his cash to build schools and hospitals, and was even elected to the Colombian Senate. But eventually the pressure got to be too much, and he turned himself in. Of course, incarceration didn't stop him from living the lush life. Escobar converted his prison into a personal fortress, even remodeling all the bathrooms and strengthening the walls. Once he left, he was a fugitive again, but he wasn't hard to track down. An obsessive germophobe, Escobar left a conspicuous trail of dilapidated hideouts with shiny, expensive new bathrooms.

G.I. JOEL

(Scrabble-playing hero)

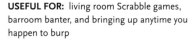

USEFUL FOR: living room Scrabble games, barroom banter, and bringing up anytime you happen to burp

KEYWORDS: Triple Word Score, bingo, or excuse me!

THE FACT: Even if you *do* know all those annoying two-letter words listed in the Official Scrabble Dictionary, you still don't stand a chance against "G.I." Joel Sherman.

In 1997, Sherman won the ridiculously competitive World Scrabble Championship in Washington, D.C., and in 2002, the National Scrabble Championship in San Diego. But that's not the only reason you want to avoid a matchup with this guy. Turns out, he didn't get his nickname because of his militaristic assaults on his opponents. Nope. The G.I. actually stands for gastrointestinal, because he belches so much during games.

instant personalities

The French poet **GERARD DE NERVAL** had a pet lobster that he enjoyed taking for walks, guiding it through the park of the Palais Royal on a pale blue ribbon.

If it wasn't for his uncle's influence, **CHARLES DARWIN** wouldn't have gone on his famous voyage on the HMS *Beagle*. The ship's captain tended to judge a man's character by his profile, and he thought so little of Darwin's nose that he initially banned him from the ship.

Who knew **GREGOR MENDEL** began his career in remedial training? That's right, the monk famous for giving peas a chance was trying to get a job teaching science in a grade school, but he failed the teaching certificate exam and was forced to take remedial biology classes.

GOD COMPLEX

(namely, Caligula's)

USEFUL FOR: impressing history professors and students of the classics, and dropping into conversations at the movie store whenever you pass the movie *Caligula*

KEYWORDS: power trip, holier than thou, or just plain loony

THE FACT: God complex or not, Caligula was immensely popular—that is, until he started declaring wars on mythological deities, literally.

Although he was emperor for just four years, Caligula (A.D. 37–41) was still able to take Rome on a wild ride, according to the ancient historians Suetonius and Flavius Josephus. The adopted son of the previous emperor, Tiberius, Caligula was initially very popular with Roman commoners. You can chalk it up to his spontaneous distributions of gold coins or his wacky, unpredictable sense of humor. Whatever the case, the public opinion quickly turned when (according to Suetonius) Caligula began cross-dressing in public, impregnated his own sister, declared war on Poseidon (bringing back chests full of worthless seashells as "booty"), and topped it all off by declaring himself a god—the classical definition of *hubris*. Poor Caligula. The seashell sovereign was assassinated by his own disgruntled bodyguards not long after.

GOLDFINGER

(the real one)

USEFUL FOR: conversing with jewelers, alchemists, and James Bond enthusiasts

KEYWORDS: gold, heists, wealthy criminals

THE FACT: British bad boy John Palmer has a cool nickname: Goldfinger. What he doesn't have is a golden rep.

Currently ranked Great Britain's wealthiest criminal, the UK scoundrel suckered over 16,000 people in a phony time-share scheme.

But that's just the start of it. Having amassed ill-gotten wealth of over £300 million, the notorious Mr. Palmer owns a fleet of cars and several houses all over England, including a huge estate at Landsdown in Bath. Palmer defended himself in the fraud trial, lost, got eight years in the clink, and has so far only been slapped with fines of £5 million. But this wasn't his first criminal activity. In 1983 he took part in the UK's greatest-ever robbery, in which he and a partner stole £26 million in gold bullion from a cargo storage company at Heathrow Airport. He smelted the gold himself and was arrested when police found two gold bars, still warm, under his sofa.

GUM CONTROL

USEFUL FOR: making conversation at precincts, with district judges, and on flights into Singapore

KEYWORDS: Hubba Bubba, Bubblicious, and gum control

THE FACT: You know the tiny nation of Singapore hates gum, but who knew the extent of their "You chews, you lose" laws?

If it weren't for the dangerously explosive nature of Pop Rocks and the counterfeiting encouraged by $100,000 bars, Singapore's classification of gum as the most evil substance on the face of the earth might come off as, oh, a tad eccentric. The ban, imposed on all citizens and tourists in 1992, emerged as a result of lawless gum chewers depositing their wads on train doors—delaying the transit system when the doors couldn't fully close. Before the laws were (sort of) relaxed in May of 2004 (permitting gum to be sold through pharmacies only, to those with proper identification) any person trying to enter Singapore with more than a few sticks could be fined $6,173 and embarrassingly locked away in jail for a year, causing those striving for a dangerous prison persona to cringe when asked, "Waddaya in for?"

HAIR LOSS

(and the magic of neutering!)

USEFUL FOR: barroom banter, conversing with bald people, and making friends with women in your Lamaze class

KEYWORDS: Rogaine, Propecia, or toupee

THE FACT: Believe it or not, the secret to baldness was discovered at a mental institution, where patients were regularly getting "fixed."

As late as 1942, male patients in some mental hospitals were castrated to quiet them. As a result, Winfield State Hospital, a mental hospital in Kansas, became a good place for Yale anatomist James Hamilton to conduct a study of castrated men. One day, one of the patients who had been stripped of his manhood received a visitor, his identical twin brother. Dr. Hamilton was struck by the fact that the brother was completely bald, while the inmate had a full head of hair. Could testosterone have something to do with baldness, the researcher wondered? To investigate this possibility Hamilton got permission to inject the castrated man with testosterone. Within six months the mental patient became as bald as his brother who had been progressively going bald over a twenty-year period. Unfortunately, the baldness was irreversible, but Dr. Hamilton had demonstrated clearly that testosterone levels could be linked to hair loss.

HAM

(as in Al Jolson, the biggest one of them all)

USEFUL FOR: cocktail parties, wrap parties, and in the middle of really bad shows you wish to God you could walk out on

KEYWORDS: show stealer, prima donna, or saving grace

THE FACT: Lots of performers have been labeled "World's Greatest Entertainer." But Jolson really, *really* believed it.

Born Asa Yoelson, Al Jolson was known for hijacking the action in the middle of shows, ad-libbing, or just stopping to talk to the audience. During a 1911 performance of the critically hated *Paris Is a Paradise for Coons* (title not edited for political correctness), Jolson stopped and asked the audience if they'd rather hear him sing than see the rest of the play. They roared their approval, and Jolson ditched the whole program and took over. From that moment on, no one else could really share the stage with him. Unlike some on this list, however, Jolson can be forgiven somewhat for his huge ego; from most contemporary accounts, he really *was* the greatest in the world. Despite the enormity of his contributions to stage and screen, Jolson's image remains a political hot potato because of his use of stage blackface (considered repellent now, but pretty acceptable at the time).

HANGOVERS

(and the easiest cure on the shelf)

USEFUL FOR: barroom banter, 21st birthdays, and convincing coworkers to go out on a work night

KEYWORDS: what're you drinking, I am so hung over, or I'm never doing that again

THE FACT: If you avoid whiskeys, and stick to the vodkas, you're bound to feel better in the morning.

Ever wonder what causes a hangover? It isn't the alcohol in the beverage. Not the alcohol that most people think of, anyway. The alcohol that intoxicates is ethanol, but the stuff responsible for the hangover is a byproduct of fermentation known as methanol. Dark wines, cognac, fruit brandies, and whiskeys contain the most methanol, while vodka has almost none. Enzymes in the body convert methanol to formaldehyde, which causes the symptoms. These enzymes actually prefer ethanol as their meal—hence the "hair of the dog" treatment for hangovers. Taking another drink provides the enzymes with ethanol, and while they gorge on this, the methanol is excreted. In the doses found in beverages, methanol may be annoying but not dangerous. In high doses methanol can intoxicate and is sometimes passed off as regular alcohol by bootleggers, and in such amounts it can be lethal.

HITCHCOCK

USEFUL FOR: cocktail parties, chatting up film buffs, assistants to stars, and people in the beef industry

KEYWORDS: Jimmy Stewart, Kim Novak, film noir, or cattle

THE FACT: There's no doubt about it: Alfred Hitchcock was without question one of the towering geniuses of cinema. But like many a genius, he kind of liked to hog the spotlight.

In fact, he was particularly trying for screenwriters, who never felt he properly credited them for their work, and notoriously hard on actors (he was very outspoken in his negative opinion of Kim Novak's performance in *Vertigo*). He was even quoted as saying, "Actors are cattle." The quip stirred up such a huge outcry (actors can be so touchy) that he issued this correction: "I have been misquoted. What I really said is: Actors should be *treated* as cattle." Although it began by accident (he was short an actor for the film *The Lodger*), he soon made it his trademark to appear in his own films, amassing a total of 37 such cameos over his career.

HORSES

(and the guy who sort of filmed them)

USEFUL FOR: impressing students of film and photography, and second-graders

KEYWORDS: animation, early photography, cinema

THE FACT: While June 15, 1878, is probably one of the most forgotten dates of all time, it's the day that made Eadweard Muybridge the Father of Motion Pictures.

The photographer was Eadweard Muybridge and the horse was Abe Edgington. Muybridge was attempting to photograph the horse running in full stride to see whether all four of the horse's hooves left the ground at the same time. Placing 12 box cameras, fitted with special tripwires 21 inches apart along the track, Muybridge essentially recorded what was too fast for the eye to see. Not only did this prove that horses become airborne while running, but the camera technique became the foundation for motion pictures. Despite a quick run-in with the law (Muybridge was also known for tracking down a journalist and shooting him for allegedly having an affair with his wife and fathering his son— later ruled a justifiable homicide), Muybridge continued to experiment with motion photography, and even earned the title Father of Motion Pictures.

HUMAN MEAT

(nutrition-wise)

USEFUL FOR: cocktail parties, bachelor parties, and chatting with vegetarians

KEYWORDS: New Guinea, cannibalism, or mad cow disease

THE FACT: You are what you eat. So it stands to reason that if you eat a diseased dead guy, you're going to become a diseased dead guy. Unfortunately, the cannibalistic Fore people of New Guinea found that out the hard way.

For most of the 20th century, the Fore were plagued by a disease called kuru, also known as the "laughing death." Kuru, a relative of mad cow disease, paralyzes its victims and causes dementia by literally creating holes in the brain. Fascinated by what he thought was a genetic disorder, scientist Daniel Carleton Gajdusek traveled to New Guinea in 1957 where he discovered that women made up the vast majority of kuru victims. He also noticed that women and children were the ones ceremonially eating the brains and intestines of dead relatives. Gajdusek deduced that the Fore were ingesting the prions, or misshapen proteins, that caused the disease. Gajdusek received a Nobel Prize for his work, and today cannibalism and kuru are all but wiped out in New Guinea.

IMELDA MARCOS

USEFUL FOR: anytime you want to feel good about spending too much on clothes

KEYWORDS: graft, corruption, or 100 percent pure evil

THE FACT: If you want to feel like a natural woman, all you need is a pair of X chromosomes. But if you want to feel like an *evil* woman, try borrowing a set from Imelda Marcos.

The former first lady of the Philippines has a biological makeup that seems like the result of a torrid love affair between Enron and Barneys. In fact, during her husband's presidency from 1965 to 1986, Imelda and Ferdinand Marcos managed to steal an estimated $3 to $35 billion from the Philippine people by siphoning foreign aid and profits from large domestic companies into their Swiss bank accounts. It's widely believed that Imelda was the mastermind behind these schemes (her children were once reportedly spotted wearing T-shirts that say, "Don't Blame My Dad. Blame My Mom!"), and her extravagant ways seemed to support this theory. Imelda is famous for her lavish jewelry and her shoes; she is said to have owned 3,000 pairs, one of which was a pair of plastic disco sandals with three-inch flashing battery-operated heels. Her contribution to her country? $28 billion in foreign debt.

INFLATION

(Boss Tweed style)

USEFUL FOR: impressing history teachers, corrupt politicians, and greedy capitalists

KEYWORDS: Tweed, overpriced, or overpriced tweed

THE FACT: The undisputed poster child of graft and greed in American politics, Boss William Tweed basically raised corruption to an art form with his (far from ethical) markups.

As a member of New York's Tammany Hall, Tweed and his cronies ran New York in the Civil War era as their own private money factory. Tweed bought 300 benches for $5 each, then sold them to the city at $600 a pop. And that's just the tip of it. The building of City Hall was a clinic in graft: the city was charged $7,500 for every thermometer, $41,190 for each broom, and $5.7 million for furniture and carpets. And although he was crooked as a dog's hind leg, Tweed does get a bit of credit from some historians for undertaking many important projects that improved life in New York (albeit at enormous financial gain to himself). Tweed's illicit profits were said to be in the range of $200 *million*, and that's in the '60s—the 1860s! The law eventually caught up with the Boss, though, and he died in prison in 1878.

INSTANT BACON

USEFUL FOR: cocktail parties, grocery store chatter, and chatting up anyone who loves their pork

KEYWORDS: kosher, pork, or mouth-watering meat in minutes

THE FACT: Any company smart enough to bless mankind with sprayable whipped cream, the sort that touts direct-to-mouth action, has got to know a thing or two about immediate gratification. Or so you'd think.

But sadly, the makers of Reddi-wip were unable to meld their keen understanding of human laziness with processed meat. The way they figured it, if you're cooking breakfast in the morning and you've got a hankering for bacon, why dirty up a pan that you'll only have to clean later? The solution— foil-wrapped Reddi Bacon you could pop into your toaster, for piping-hot pork in seconds. What's more, the stuff actually tasted pretty good! Too bad the brains behind the bacon forgot that bacon grease turns to liquid when heated. Tragically, the Reddi Bacon foil wrappers leaked, creating a definite fire hazard, a messy (if not totally ruined) toaster, and a product that lasted about as long as it took to cook.

instant personalities

BEN FRANKLIN loved working in the nude. It's true: Almost every morning, big Ben would take an "air bath," waking up early in the morning, stripping down, opening his window for a cool breeze, and then penning his thoughts for half an hour or so.

Talk about a sore sport! Believe it or not, famed Italian artist **CARAVAGGIO** once killed a man while arguing over the score of a tennis match.

PRESIDENT DWIGHT D. EISENHOWER was an avid golfer and actually had a putting green put on the White House lawn. When a bunch of squirrels damaged his addition, he went "Caddyshack" on them, and issued an executive order to have them expelled.

INTERSTATE HIGHWAYS

(and why Hawaii has 'em)

USEFUL FOR: cocktail parties, road trips, and telling anyone who'll listen

KEYWORDS: why does Hawaii have interstate highways

THE FACT: While we'd like to believe Hawaii's interstate highway system exists for the sole purpose of annoying George Carlin, there's a simple reason behind it.

Like it or not, the "interstate" name is actually a misnomer. The truth is that not all interstates physically go from one state to another; the name merely implies that the roads receive federal funding. As for three Hawaii interstates (H-1, H-2, and H-3), they became Interstates as part of the Dwight D. Eisenhower System of Interstate and National Defense Highways. The sweeping initiative to build better highways from state to state was actually a defense measure meant to protect the U.S. from a Soviet invasion by making it easier to get supplies from one military base to another. Interstate H-201 (formerly state route 78) joined the other three in July 2004.

IRELAND

(and that whole potato famine)

USEFUL FOR: barroom banter, impressing your econ professor, and chatting up anyone in the baked potato fix-it line

KEYWORDS: potatoes, blarney, or luck of the Irish

THE FACT: You might think of the potato crisis as a punch line, but due to its effects, only half as many people live in Ireland as did before the famine.

Until the late 1800s, economic crisis usually meant agricultural crisis, with famine a not-so-infrequent consequence. Before the advent of industrial agricultural methods, weather conditions and infestations of various kinds had the power to hold the economy hostage. In 1845 a new fungus that isn't really a fungus, *Phytophthora infestans*, struck the potato—the mainstay of Ireland's food supply. Although the blight lasted only a few years, its effects were far-reaching. As many as 1.5 million died as a direct result of the famine, and many more emigrated in the second half of the 19th century. And like we said, even today only half as many people live in the nation as did before the great potato crisis.

JAPANESE DIETS

(for putting on the pounds)

USEFUL FOR: barroom banter, impressing wrestlers and giving carb counters nightmares

KEYWORDS: sumo, diet, fat, or Weight Watchers

THE FACT: Like nearly every aspect of sumo life, the famed Japanese wrestlers' diet is based on centuries of tradition. So what exactly makes up this traditional chow?

Oddly enough, sumos put on their enormous weight—700 pounds and more—mostly by consuming a simple diet of *chankonabe*, a thick boiled stew containing tofu, carrots, cabbages, leeks, potatoes, lotus roots, daikon radishes, shiitake mushrooms, and giant burdock in chicken broth. Some recipes call for shrimp, noodles, raw eggs, or beer. Doesn't sound particularly fattening, does it? In fact, *chankonabe* is quite healthy, high in both protein and vitamins. But three factors play into the whole weight-gaining aspect of it for sumo: 1) they eat a lot of it—an *awful* lot of it, 2) sumo traditionally skip breakfast, consuming most of their calories at an enormous midday meal, after which 3) they immediately take a three- or four-hour nap. As most nutritionists will tell you, skipping breakfast and then sleeping immediately after a meal is a guaranteed way to pack on the pounds.

JEFFERSON

(and the ladies)

USEFUL FOR: making small talk at reenactments and political fund-raisers, and helping debunk anyone who talks reverently about the Founding Fathers

KEYWORDS: Sally Hemings, the Constitution, presidential affairs

THE FACT: Known for his extreme intellect and skills at diplomacy, Thomas Jefferson is truly one of America's Founding Fathers, but in more ways than for his patriotism.

Considered a loving and faithful husband to Martha during their ten years of marriage before her death, Tom Jefferson was actually a bit of a tom cat. While on a trip to New York in 1768, John Walker asked Tom to look after his wife and that he did, literally. Later in 1786 as ambassador to France, Jefferson fell deeply in love with Maria Conway, the wife of portraitist Richard Conway. Legend has it that one day, while walking through the countryside, Tom tried to show off for the blushing (Conway) bride and fell while jumping a fence only to break his wrist. But Tom's best-known relationship was with Sally Hemings, his slave and his late wife's half sister. Their relationship went on for 35 years and provided Jefferson a number of heirs. Ironically, Jefferson detested interracial relationships and never gave Sally her freedom.

JELL-O

(and its long war)

USEFUL FOR: impressing biology teachers, six-year-olds, and Grandma

KEYWORDS: Jell-O mold, pineapples, or Bill Cosby

THE FACT: We've seen the end of a cold war, Republicans dance with Democrats, little black and white kids walk hand in hand . . . so why is it that Jell-O and pineapples still won't get along?

If Jell-O ads and 1950s cookbooks are to be believed, you can mix almost *anything* with gelatin and have it come out tasty. Ham? Absolutely. Carrots? Sure thing. Tomato soup? Mm, mm good. The only ingredient that seems to be taboo is one that actually sounds delicious: fresh pineapple. Unfortunately, the tropical treat works like kryptonite on Jell-O because it contains an enzyme called bromelain, which prevents gelatin from forming into a solid. But fret not, congealed salad fans: *Canned* pineapple doesn't contain bromelain. The canning process heats the pineapple to a temperature sufficient to break the enzyme down, making it oh so Jell-O friendly.

JESUS' BROTHERS

USEFUL FOR: questioning your pastor, Sunday school debate, taunting your younger sibling into believing they'll be similarly forgotten

KEYWORDS: sibling rivalry, Virgin Mary, or Son of God

THE FACT: The New Testament mentions brothers (*adelphoi* in Greek) of Jesus and even names them. Yet somehow history still depicts him as an only child.

Most historians would go so far as to say the *adelphoi* James, Simon, Judas (different from apostles James, Simon, and Judas), and Joseph were Jesus' cousins. And it's true, according to Catholic theology: Jesus' mother, Mary, never had sexual intercourse and never bore a child other than the Messiah, so the *adelphoi* couldn't have been his brothers. Other lines of thought, though, tell it a little differently, claiming that the Gospel writers used *adelphoi* literally and that Mary was a virgin only until after the birth of J.C. We don't want to take sides, but if these four guys really were Jesus' brothers, they got the seriously short end of the sibling stick. Imagine! Not only is your brother God Almighty, he's also the most famous man in history. Meanwhile, scholars are sitting around arguing about whether you ever even existed.

JEWS

(in Ethiopia?)

USEFUL FOR: breaking stereotypes, impressing religion majors, and making it sound like you're well versed on African history

KEYWORDS: kosher, matzo, or Ethiopia

THE FACT: Most of the people of the central highlands of Ethiopia, numbering more than 25 million, speak Semitic languages that are more closely related to Hebrew than they are to the other languages of sub-Saharan ("south of the Sahara") Africa.

Sounds strange, but it's definitely true. The central Ethiopians, moreover, began practicing Christianity roughly 1,700 years ago, much earlier than did the people of northern Europe. Until recently, Ethiopia also had a thriving Jewish community, that of the Falashas. The Falashas had long been isolated from other Jewish groups, and as a result they held only a small portion of the Jewish Holy Scriptures. A debate ensued over whether they should therefore be considered true Jews. Once the issue was decided in the affirmative, virtually the entire community migrated to Israel.

KIM JONG IL

USEFUL FOR: chatting up immigrants, impressing history teachers, and determining the number one place you'll never want to take your family on vacation

KEYWORDS: North Korea, dictators, and King Kong (who's bigger than Kim Jong, but hardly badder)

THE FACT: If you really want to escape globalization, you might try sneaking into North Korea. Of course, you'll probably be arrested . . .

. . . and executed, and you may even be captured and eaten by villagers. (Between one and three million North Koreans have starved to death over the past decade, and incidents of cannibalism have been regularly reported.) But if you do survive the ordeal, you can bear witness to the most extravagant personality cult in history, one that makes the efforts of Hitler, Stalin, and Saddam Hussein look rather modest in comparison. Kim Il Sung, the country's founding dictator, is still its official president—even though he died in 1994. (Why be president for life when you can have the position for all eternity?) His son, Kim Jong Il, now the country's "dear leader," is evidently doing his best to follow in his father footsteps.

KITTY-CAT

(and her high jump)

USEFUL FOR: not freaking out whenever
Scratchy tries to dive off the mantel

KEYWORDS: cat, suicidal, or high dive

THE FACT: Furry felines have a knack for
jumping from high places and only getting the
wind knocked out them (helps with the hairballs).

It helps that kitties are lightweights, and can twist around
and land on all fours. Their superbalance has something to
do with their inner ears, and luck (unless they're black cats,
of course). And here's the weirdest part: Kitties actually have
a better chance of surviving a fall from a higher place than a
low one. When they jump off tall buildings (instead of short
treehouses) they achieve what's called a terminal velocity—
the point at which they stop accelerating. Once they hit the
"TV" zone, they can relax a bit, enjoy the ride, and spread
their paws to make a parachute. Then again, they may just
have nine lives . . .

KLACKERS

USEFUL FOR: scaring kids, scaring moms, and delighting anyone looking for some eye patch nostalgia

KEYWORDS: bullies, nerds, or "that toy is not a weapon"

THE FACT: Klackers were basically the definition of a mother's warning: all fun and games until kids lost some eyes.

In the late 1960s, a toy called Klackers hit the market. The pendulum-like device was made up of two large balls or marbles attached to a string hanging from a ring or handle. The goal was to get the hanging balls to tap together by pulling up with your hand. And if you got really good at it, you could get them clacking against each other extremely fast, both above and below your hand. Klackers became wildly popular, but in 1971, the toy was yanked from store shelves after a rash of Klacker-related injuries. Apparently, kids who were not so good at the game were getting bruises and black eyes from errant balls. Other kids reported similar injuries, not from *playing* with Klackers, but having them used against them by bullies. Most injuries, however, occurred when the clacking balls (which, brilliantly enough, were sometimes made of glass) shattered and sent Klacker shrapnel into the eyes of hundreds of children.

KLUTZINESS

(and the inventions it spurs)

USEFUL FOR: chatting up inventors, making small talk in the ER, and anytime you want to make your clumsy spouse feel better

KEYWORDS: Band-Aids, inventors, or klutz

THE FACT: It's like they say—behind every great man is a woman who burns herself a lot.

It all started in 1920, when Johnson & Johnson employee Earle Dickson wed his sweetheart, Josephine, and discovered that she wasn't exactly Little Mary Homemaker. Turns out she had a rather unnerving habit of kitchen klutziness. Every day, Dickson would come home to find another cut or burn that needed dressing. He was sympathetic at first, but as time passed, the score increased to Kitchen: 500, Josephine: 0, and he grew more frustrated. Finally, Dickson came up with a way for his wife to fix her wounds without having to wait for him by taking a roll of surgical tape and spacing out squares of gauze down the length of it. To keep the tape from sticking to itself, he added a layer of removable crinoline. Forever after, when Josephine injured herself, she simply peel a length from the roll and patched it up, and thus, Band-Aids were born. No word on the final outcome of Josephine versus the Kitchen, but we're hoping no news is good news.

KOALAS

(with VD!)

USEFUL FOR: cocktail parties, trips to the zoo, and lecturing your kids about bear safety

KEYWORDS: protection, condoms, or cuddly

THE FACT: While koalas are pretty well known for sleeping, they should also be well known for sleeping around!

While few animals are as cute as the cuddly koala, they wouldn't be much fun as pets. Koalas sleep up to 16 hours a day and aren't all that peppy when they're awake. Maybe that's because stressed-out koalas are particularly prone to chlamydia. Yes, *that* chlamydia. The widespread STD among Koalas makes them prone to conjunctivitis ("pink eye"), urinary tract infections (no quick runs to the grocery store for some cranberry juice for these guys!), and incontinence. Which, by the way, is not only a reason not to have one as a pet, but also a reason to forgo the requisite "koala-holding picture" on your trip to Australia.

Though the White House had needed extensive repairs ever since British troops had set it on fire in 1814, reconstruction didn't begin until the late 1940s with **PRESIDENT HARRY TRUMAN**, when he witnessed a piano fall through the floor.

What's worse than forgetting to turn off your ringer at a somber event? Forgetting to turn off your pet. At **ANDREW JACKSON**'s funeral in 1845, his parrot had to be removed for swearing so much.

Talk about bizarre morning rituals: **PRESIDENT CALVIN COOLIDGE** liked having his head rubbed with petroleum jelly while he feasted on breakfast in bed.

KUDZU

(Japan's worst export)

USEFUL FOR: cocktail party banter, chatting up botanists, and sparking road-trip conversation across the southland

KEYWORDS: invincible, unwanted, or kudzu

THE FACT: In 1876, the fast-growing vine kudzu made its way from Japan to the United States and quickly became all the rage. Little did people know how quickly the plant was going to wear out its welcome.

In the South, its heavy coverage provided shade from the heat, the livestock seemed to like the taste, and it even improved the quality of the soil. Kudzu seemed to have so many advantages, in fact, that in the 1930s the U.S. government helped farmers plant the vine all across the Southern states. Big mistake. Less than 20 years later, the kudzu had spread out of control, covering crop fields and trees, often killing the vegetation in its path. Today utility companies in the South spend millions of dollars trying to keep their poles and towers kudzu-free with no help from the U.S. government other than a list of vine-ridding tips on its Web site. Gee, thanks, Uncle Sam!

LANGUAGE ARTS

(in Papua New Guinea)

USEFUL FOR: armchair travelers, people planning trips, and chatting up linguists and missionaries

KEYWORDS: pidgin, PNG, or if you don't speak the language . . .

THE FACT: If you're going to Papua New Guinea, you'll probably need a translator, if not a few hundred of 'em.

No country has more linguistic diversity than Papua New Guinea (PNG). More than 800 languages are currently spoken in the country, and no one linguistic group contains more than a small percentage of the population. In fact, many languages of the interior are poorly known, although missionary linguists are working hard to record them in preparation for Bible translation. So how does Papua New Guinea function as a country, considering this welter of tongues? Some form of common speech is necessary, and PNG has one in English. Well, not exactly English as we know it, rather Melanesian pidgin English, based on a simplified vocabulary and local grammatical and sound structures. Thus, a foreign tourist would generally be labeled a *man bilong longwe ples* (or "man belong long-way place").

LA-Z-BOY

(and the genius who came up with it)

USEFUL FOR: lazy afternoons, justifying a thoroughly inactive lifestyle, or convincing yourself exercise isn't the key

KEYWORDS: lazy, genius, and lazy genius

THE FACT: Edwin Shoemaker was a genius (and we don't throw that word around lightly). After all, the guy forever blurred the distinction between sitting up and lying down by developing the world's first reclining chair. Even more impressive: He was only 21 years old at the time.

Edwin Shoemaker came up with the concept back in 1928! Who knew a lazy kid with a lazy dream could make all that laziness work out so well? Of course, Fast Eddy's initial model, a wood-slat chair intended for porches, wasn't exactly the most comfortable thing in the world. It was fashioned out of orange crates and designed to fit the contours of the back at any angle. It took an early customer, appreciative of the concept but rather unexcited about the prospect of lying down on bare slats of wood, to suggest *upholstering* the invention. Shoemaker and his partner Edward Knabusch then held a contest to name the invention. "La-Z-Boy" beat out suggestions like "Sit 'n' Snooze" and "The Slack-Back."

LEMMINGS

USEFUL FOR: impressing your fourth-grade teacher, or any seven-year old who'll listen to you

KEYWORDS: lemmings, suicide, or lemming suicides

THE FACT: Lemmings don't intentionally jump off cliffs—they do it because they're morons.

Poor, oft-maligned lemmings—you couldn't blame them for being suicidal, if they were, which they aren't. So where exactly did the myth come from? The notion of lemming suicide extends back to at least to Freud, who in 1929's *Civilization and Its Discontents* explained the human death instinct in the context of the creatures. But the notion didn't really take hold until Walt Disney's 1958 so-called documentary *White Wilderness* hit the big screen. For the purpose of his film, the lovable animator shipped dozens of lemmings to Alberta, Canada, herded them off a cliff, taped them falling to their deaths, and passed it off as nonfiction. In reality, though, lemmings aren't suicidal. They're just dumb. The truth is, lemming populations explode in four-year cycles in Scandinavia, and when the tundra gets crowded, they seek out new land. Being stupid, they sometimes fall off cliffs, but not on purpose.

LEONARDO DA VINCI

(da genius, da Italian, da bastard?)

USEFUL FOR: cocktail parties, academic gatherings, and basically impressing anyone who's ever heard of Leonardo da Vinci

KEYWORDS: da Vinci, mistake, and Planned Parenthood

THE FACT: Everyone knows of Leonardo da Vinci, the *homo universalis* who was a painter, a naturalist, a metallurgist, and a philosopher with equal ease. But not everyone knows he was basically the product of a one-afternoon stand.

It's true! The personification of the Renaissance was actually the son of a notary, Ser Piero, and a peasant girl of somewhat "easy virtue." In fact, the two simply took a tumble in the hay together before going their separate ways and providing Leonardo, from their marriages with other people, with 17 half brothers and sisters. Needless to say, these assorted half siblings were none too fond of their renowned relation, whose birth was something of an embarrassment, and on his father's death, in 1503, they conspired to deprive him of his share of the estate. Leonardo had the last laugh, however, when the death of an uncle led to a similar inheritance squabble, leaving him with sole custody of the uncle's lands and property.

LEONA HELMSLEY

USEFUL FOR: cocktail parties, punch lines, and tours of the Empire State Building

KEYWORDS: Leona Helmsley, immigrant, tax evasion

THE FACT: Believe it or not, the famous New York real estate mogul and class A witch actually lived the American Dream. Well, except for the whole prison thing.

Leona was a divorced sewing factory worker with mouths to feed before she met and married real estate tycoon Harry Helmsley. In 1980, Harry named Leona president of his opulent Helmsley Palace Hotel, which she ruled like a despot. Her tendency to explode at employees for the smallest infraction (like a crooked lampshade) earned her the title "The Queen of Mean." The tyranny didn't exactly last. In 1988 Leona and Harry were indicted for a smorgasbord of crimes, including tax fraud, mail fraud, and extortion. She served 18 months in prison and was forced to pay the government $7 million in back taxes. That doesn't mean things turned out that badly for poor Leona. Said to be worth over $2.2 billion, the dreaded Ms. H still owns the lease to the Empire State Building and lives in luxury with her aptly named dog, Trouble.

LICKS

(to the center of a Tootsie Pop)

USEFUL FOR: Halloween parties, chatting up people nostalgic for the '70s, and blowing the minds of seven-year olds across the globe

KEYWORDS: owl, lick, or Tootsie Pop

THE FACT: No thanks to that pesky owl and his woeful lack of willpower, the "How Many Licks Does It Take to Get to the Tootsie Roll Center of a Tootsie Pop?" question has been plaguing the American public ever since the commercial first aired in 1970.

Fortunately, there have been plenty of noble efforts to get to the bottom (or center, as the case may be) of it all. But the answer depends on whom you ask. A group of students at Swarthmore Junior High conducted an extensive study on the subject and concluded that getting to the center of a Tootsie Pop took a statistical average of 144 licks. However, the more ambitious and distrusting engineering students at Purdue University chose instead to rely on a "licking machine," modeled after the human tongue for their results. The Boilermakers and their mechanical contraption found that it requires an average of 364 licks. Other studies have been done, and all results vary, so only one thing is certain: The world may never know.

LIONS

(and one particularly sexy beast)

USEFUL FOR: cocktail parties, chatting up
scientists, making friends at the fertility clinic

KEYWORDS: virility, fertility, sex fiends, or the
zoo

THE FACT: Despite his world wide rep, Frasier,
the Sensuous Lion, didn't actually do much
bragging about his amorous exploits. Then
again, he didn't have to—his proof was walking
all around him!

Here's how the story goes: Frasier was about 20 years old,
ancient for a lion, when he came to a wild animal park in
southern California. Unfortunately, the Mexican circus refugee
was so doddering that he could hardly walk, and his keepers
simply figured his demise would be any day. But that didn't
stop the old lion from tomcatting about. Frasier hung on for 18
months and sired a stunning 35 cubs in his spare time.
Amazingly, the press about the fertile feline was so widespread
that Frasier fan clubs started sprouting up everywhere. Wives
even began writing in to find out what park rangers were
feeding the beast. In fact, the lion's fame grew so much that a
popular song was written about him, and a film was made as
well. When the old cat's time finally came, it's said, Frasier, the
Sensuous Lion, went with a smile on his face.

LIQUID PAPER

USEFUL FOR: making friends with people at Staples, OfficeMax, and Kinko's

KEYWORDS: whiteout, mistakes, and typewriters

THE FACT: The woman behind Liquid Paper, Bette Nesmith Graham, wasn't just a sloppy typist turned secretary extraordinaire. She's also "Mom" to former Monkees member, Michael Nesmith (the tall one with the funny hat).

It all started when Graham joined a typing pool in 1951. Recently divorced, she desperately needed the job to support herself and her as-yet-unprimatelike son. Problem was, typing wasn't exactly her forte, and she became increasingly worried that her frequent errors would get her fired. Then inspiration struck. Graham filled a nail polish bottle with white tempera paint and took it to work. Whenever she made a mistake, she simply painted over it. Before long, the whole typing pool was indulging. As demand for what Graham first called "Mistake Out" grew, it began to distract her from her secretarial duties. In 1962, she was fired for using company time to write letters for her own business, but that turned out to be just the push Graham needed. Within six years, Liquid Paper was a million-dollar business, and Graham was laughing all the way to the bank.

LORD OF THE (CIGAR) RINGS

USEFUL FOR: barroom banter, making friends in cigar shops, and bringing up at Sunday school

KEYWORDS: Cubans, smoking or, oh, my God!

THE FACT: In the highlands of Guatemala, you're likely to run in to members of the cult of Maximón, a Maya group that worships its cigar-chomping deity in a rather unusual way.

Worshippers believe Maximón, also known as San Simon, is a powerful saint who possesses the ability to, among other things, cure illnesses and confront Christ. Different shrines and chapels in Guatemala have different effigies built to represent Maximón, but a few things are pretty consistent: His face is made from wood, he's got a (lit) cigar hanging from his mouth, and he's surrounded by bottles of liquor. In some places, he may be nothing more than a wooden box with a cigarette sticking out of it; in others, he might be sporting sunglasses or a bandanna. Either way, if you see him, just be sure you have the proper offering. In exchange for blessings, he accepts cigarettes (Payaso brand are his favorite) and most any rum (although he's partial to Venado).

LOSING A BET

(the tale of Stephen Hawking)

USEFUL FOR: nerdy dates, academic gatherings, proving even geniuses make mistakes (and buy porn)

KEYWORDS: physics, *Penthouse*, or Hawking

THE FACT: One tiny mistake and the world's most famous physicists ended up buying a subscription to one of the world's raunchiest publications.

Well known for authoring *A Brief History of Time*, the world-renowned theoretician has made his greatest contributions in the physics of black holes. He was also elected one of the Royal Society's youngest fellows and selected to Cambridge's Lucasian post, a professorship of mathematics once held by Isaac Newton. While all signs point to genius, that doesn't mean Hawking is always right. Earlier in his career, he made a bet with Kip Thorne of Caltech that Cygnus X-1 did not contain a black hole. (The prize was a subscription to a racy magazine.) In 1990, when Hawking decided the evidence against him was overwhelming, he conceded in a waggish manner: He had a friend break into Thorne's office and steal the recorded terms of the bet—Hawkings signed his defeat, then snuck it back in for Thorne to find later. In the following months, Thorne also received his promised issues of *Penthouse*.

THE LOTTO

(Founding Father style)

USEFUL FOR: cocktail parties, convenience store lines, convincing ultrapatriotic Americans that the Powerball isn't immoral (at least according to the Framers)

KEYWORDS: Founding Fathers, lucky numbers, or Powerball

THE FACT: Despite what you may think about lotteries, early American leaders often turned to them to raise a buck or two.

It's completely true! Displaying the astute politicians' aversion to direct taxation, John Hancock organized several lotteries, including one to rebuild Boston's Faneuil Hall. Ben Franklin used them during the Revolutionary War to purchase a cannon for the Continental Army. George Washington ran a lottery to pay for a road into the wilds of western Virginia. And Thomas Jefferson wrote of lotteries that "far from being immoral, they are indispensable to the existence of man." Of course when he wrote it, he was trying to convince the Virginia legislature to let him hold a lottery to pay off his debts.

LOVE LETTERS

(to a pigeon)

USEFUL FOR: cocktail parties, chatting up scientists, and making small talk whenever you and your loved ones are kicking pigeons in the park

KEYWORDS: AC/DC, true love, or pigeons

THE FACT: Who knew that Nikola Tesla, one of physics' greatest minds, had such a penchant for chicks (we're talking about the feathered kind)?

Tesla dreamed up AC current, won technical disputes with Edison, had ideas stolen from him by Marconi, and designed the Tesla coil (that lovely spinning thing you find sparking light in every mad scientist's lab). But even more intriguing than all of this were his peculiarities. Nikola Tesla's personal life was one of crippling obsessions: washing his hands endlessly, counting every item on a dinner table before tucking in, and maintaining a hatred for earrings and other round objects. But perhaps most unusual was his fondness for pigeons. Tesla was so smitten by one bird in particular that when it passed away, he wrote, "Yes, I loved her as a man loves a woman, and she loved me . . . When that pigeon died something went out of my life . . . I knew my life's work was over."

instant personalities

Race car driver **DICK TRICKLE** is a perennial Winston Cup loser (he's never won the event despite 300-plus career attempts through 2004), though he clearly isn't too focused on his driving. Dick once requested a lighter be installed in his car so he could smoke mid-race.

Author **VICTOR HUGO** had an unusual solution for writer's block. He had his servant take away his clothes with strict orders not to return them for several hours. Left buck naked, and with nothing else to do, Hugo was forced to return to his pen and paper.

STEPHEN HAWKING was famous among his schoolmates for being terrible with electronics. He once attempted to turn an old television into an amplifier and gave himself a 500-volt shock.

THE MAD HATTER

(a slightly more gangsterish one than Alice met)

USEFUL FOR: costume parties, impressing your history teacher, inciting mob nostalgia with your friends in Witness Protection

KEYWORDS: nicknames, gangsters, or fancy hats

THE FACT: One of history's strangest nicknamed mafiosos in the world, Albert "Lord High Executioner" Anastasia was also dubbed "The Mad Hatter" for his love of fancy fedoras.

As the whole "Lord High Executioner" name suggests, Al wasn't exactly a man to be messed with. In the early 1920s, Anastasia was sentenced to death for killing a fellow longshoreman. But he was granted a retrial and the conviction was reversed when four of the witnesses "disappeared." And that was just at the start of his career. After helping to kill crime boss Joe Masseria, Anastasia was made head of Murder, Inc. by new boss Lucky Luciano, and was dubbed the Mob's "Lord High Executioner" by the press. And while the name stuck, his position didn't, as Anastasia eventually fell out with the other bosses. On October 25, 1957, Anastasia was shot six times while getting a haircut. As one New York paper put it the next day: "He Died in the Chair After All."

MARQUIS DE SADE

USEFUL FOR: barroom banter, bachelor parties, and generally impolite company

KEYWORDS: sadism, sadomasochism, and de Sade

THE FACT: How great would it be to have sadism named after you? Of course, you'd have to go to certain lengths, as the Marquis definitely did.

Essentially pawned off by his family, the Marquis de Sade was married to a woman for the money. Choosing to fulfill the "for worse" part of the whole marriage vow deal, he immediately began to busy himself (quite publicly) with prostitutes, and with a sister-in-law. Of course, de Sade's mother-in-law didn't like that, and she had him imprisoned. So he spent 14 years in jail, including being condemned to death in the town of Aix for his sexual practices. Yet somehow he got out of that one. Then he was imprisoned again in 1777, and again for six years at the Bastille in Paris in 1784. Imprisonment gave him lots of time to keep churning out the vigorous pornography that made him famous. In fact, the Marquis spent his last 12 years in the insane asylum at Charenton, where he wrote and directed plays starring the staff and inmates.

MASTICATION

(it's not a dirty word)

USEFUL FOR: dinner parties, cocktail parties, and parties where you get stuck at the kids' table

KEYWORDS: chew your food

THE FACT: Also called "the Chew-Chew Man," American importer and art dealer Horace Fletcher gained a huge following when he began donning a white jacket, and lecturing and writing about nutrition. His 1890s theme: Chew.

So what made him so popular? Fletcher advised that nothing should be swallowed unless it could be reduced to liquid first by chewing. Supported by studies that found chewing every morsel 32 times could be beneficial for weight loss (it slowed down the rate of eating, at the very least), Fletcher claimed such adherents as novelist Henry James and industrialist John D. Rockefeller. Health reformer Dr. John Harvey Kellogg was also a devotee of "Fletcherizing" for a while, and even made up a "chewing song" for patients. Of course, keeping to the philosophy wasn't all roses. Many Fletcherizers spit out anything they could not chew to liquid, which eliminated a lot of dietary fiber and led to constipation.

MATZO BALLS

(you should probably pass over)

USEFUL FOR: cocktail parties, barroom banter, and daring anyone to repeat the feat

KEYWORDS: Matzo, Passover, dreidl, or all you can eat

THE FACT: It ain't easy keeping kosher. Especially for contestants in Ben's Kosher Delicatessen Charity Matzo Ball Eating Contest (where even the name's a mouthful).

The contest is a charity fund-raiser for the Interfaith Nutrition Network by a New York–area deli chain. The 2004 record holder is Eric "Badlands" Booker of Copaigue, Long Island, who ate 20 1/4 matzo balls in five minutes and 25 seconds. If that doesn't sound like a lot, you should know that these matzo balls were roughly the size of *tennis* balls. *Oy!* The winner gets a trophy and a $2,500 gift certificate to a stereo store, while runners-up get various prize packages, all of which involve tickets to a New York Islanders game. Umm . . . all that matzo for an Islanders ticket? We're thinking we'll pass.

MERCEDES-BENZ

(and the women who really love 'em)

USEFUL FOR: cocktail parties, nerdy dates, and making small talk at Mercedes-Benz dealerships

KEYWORDS: anytime you hear the word R-E-S-P-E-C-T spelled out in song

THE FACT: Apparently, the Mercedes-Benz as a status symbol doesn't just cross highways, it crosses cultures as well. Case in point: the Nanas women of Togo in Africa.

The Nanas represent a stunning rags-to-riches story, overcoming illiteracy and cultural barriers when they cornered the lucrative cloth trade. After acquiring loans and making a few sharp investments, these women now conduct multimillion-dollar international transactions. In fact, the Nanas' have expanded their businesses to hair salons, bakeries, restaurants, and real estate. What's the Nanas' status symbol of choice? The Benz, of course. So many of the Nanas drive around in them, in fact, that the most successful are known as Nana-Benz. The Nanas, however, aren't the only group in Africa to incorporate the Mercedes moniker into their name. The WaBenzi, a powerful and elite class of people in many African nations, got its name because of its members' favorite car. WaBenzi loosely translates to "people of Mercedes-Benz."

MICE
(and men)

USEFUL FOR: barroom banter, irritating members of PETA, and chatting up Australians

KEYWORDS: mice, *Fear Factor*, or sushi

THE FACT: Sure, the MTV show *Jackass* spawned a lot of moronic copycats, but two hungry fellas in Brisbane, Australia, win the prize for trying to down a live mouse.

It's disturbingly true. Participating in a contest at Brisbane's Exchange Hotel in which they were dared to eat the rodents live, the winner's grand prize was a vacation package worth a handsome $346. Both men chewed the tails off, and the "winner" actually chewed his mouse whole and spit it out. Needless to say, the RSPCA, Australia's version of our own SPCA, wasn't thrilled about the stunt and got the Queensland police on the participants' . . . um . . . tail. If caught, the winner will face fines of $75,000 and two years in the pokey. Where there will no doubt be plenty of big, fat, edible rodents for snacking on.

MICROWAVES

(and the guy you should thank for 'em)

USEFUL FOR: movie theater chatter, making small talk while waiting for your popcorn to pop, and impressing anyone who really loves their microwave

KEYWORDS: I really love my microwave

THE FACT: If it weren't for the candy bar in Percy Spencer's pocket, it might have been years before we got the kitchen appliance.

Radar and microwave technologies developed during World War II were credited with helping to change the tide in the battle in Europe. But after the war, scientists like Percy Spencer stumbled across all sorts of new applications for the technology. Percy, who was working for Raytheon at the time, happened to be in the path of powerful radiation emitted from a magnetron (ouch), when he noticed that the candy bar in his pocket had melted. He then put popcorn kernels in front of the device and watched in fascination as the popcorn popped. He also demonstrated cooking an egg from the inside out (don't do this at home, they tend to explode!). Of course, using low-density microwave energy to cook is now commonplace, and Spencer's use of popcorn as an early experimental substance was prescient—today the United States produces 500,000 tons of popcorn, most of which is cooked in microwave ovens.

MILK

(it does a reputation good)

USEFUL FOR: barroom banter, fraternity halls, wherever someone is carrying a funnel and a six-pack

KEYWORDS: got milk, milk mustache, or really anytime the word *milk* comes up

THE FACT: Before civil wars ravaged Sudan, unmarried Dinka tribesmen used to compete in extreme milk-drinking competitions to strut their stuff for eligible females.

The goal was for the men to gulp down endless gallons of the stuff and refrain from exercise in an effort to become as fat as possible. Supposedly, this showed the single ladies that a bachelor had enough cattle to drink all this extra milk. Of course, this isn't the only case where excessive weight is associated with stature. Various cultures throughout history, from South Asian to Polynesian societies, have valued obesity as an indicator of the lush life. Dinka men, however, are generally quite tall and thin (basketball star Manute Bol being one of the more prominent), and some men would gain so many unfamiliar milk pounds so quickly that they were known to topple over upon rising from the competition.

MONA LISA

(gone missing)

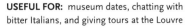

USEFUL FOR: museum dates, chatting with bitter Italians, and giving tours at the Louvre

KEYWORDS: Leonardo da Vinci, Italian pride, or bumbling art heist

THE FACT: While the *Mona Lisa*'s probably pretty well protected today, there used to be a time when you could walk into the Louvre and just pluck it off the wall. In fact, somebody did.

In 1911, an Italian workman named Vincenzo Peruggia walked into the gallery, took the painting off the wall, and carried it out. Not exactly the high-minded cat burglary you might imagine, since security was practically nonexistent. Of course, it did take officials about two years before they located Old Mona buried in a trunk in Vincenzo's cheap lodging in Florence. So what was the working man's motive? Not money apparently. Vinnie claimed that since the painting was by an Italian, Leonardo da Vinci, it was part of Italy's national cultural heritage, and he was, in true patriotic spirit, simply taking it back to where it belonged: Florence. The painting was returned to the Louvre shortly thereafter.

MONOGAMY

(a.k.a. A Tale of Two Georges)

USEFUL FOR: impressing your history teacher or date, or arguing that monogamy and true love actually might not be myths

KEYWORDS: mistress, low fidelity, or royal romance (sort of)

THE FACT: While most royalty has a real problem with the whole "staying faithful" thing, a couple of Georges were apparently cast from a different mold.

From harems to courtesans, it can make you dizzy to think about all the women on the side royal men have taken a "liking to." Oddly enough, though, there have been a few kings who wanted desperately to be faithful to their beloveds. Take England's King George II (1683–1760) for example. Old George was happily married to his wife, Queen Caroline, but he took a mistress just to *maintain his reputation*. After all, a mistressless king could be seen as weak or, worse still, impotent. His son, George III, however, broke that streak of monarchial infidelity when he married the notoriously homely Princess Charlotte Sophia in 1761. Seeing her for the first time, George is said to have winced in disgust, but the two came to love one another immensely (and frequently—they had 15 kids), and George III was never unfaithful.

MOTHS

(that use protection)

USEFUL FOR: barroom banter, chatting up etymologists

KEYWORDS: stamina, moths, or unusual types of protection

THE FACT: If you're looking for clever dating tactics, put down your men's magazine and take a closer look at the male red moth of the *Cosmosoma myrodora* species.

The male red moth dines on the fluid from the leaves of the dog fennel plant and stores some of it in a pair of pouches under his abdomen. Then, when the little guy goes a-courting, he discharges the pouch contents all over the female, sort of like nuptial confetti. The fluid contains a variety of alkaloids from the plant that repel predators, such as spiders. Indeed, virgin female moths coated with the stuff and placed into spiders' webs are quickly cut loose by the spider. This chemical protection seems vital since the moths spend up to nine hours copulating! The male wants to ensure that his mate doesn't become a meal while he attempts to impregnate her.

MOUNT EVEREST

(and the guy who should've gotten credit)

USEFUL FOR: cocktail parties, impressing your history teacher, consoling anyone who's ever felt shafted

KEYWORDS: Everest, Sir Edmund Hillary

THE FACT: While Hillary gets all the glory for getting to the top of Everest first, he should probably share some of the hype with his Nepalese buddy who got him there.

Tenzing Norgay was a Sherpa, one of the hardy mountain folk of Nepal. Like many Sherpa, he discovered that he could make a nice living guiding Europeans up the mountains of his homeland. In 1953, he led Sir John Hunt's expedition to Mount Everest, the highest point on earth. But few remember Norgay's name, because a New Zealander, Edmund Hillary, insisted on being the first person to stand on the summit. It took Hillary and company seven weeks to climb to the summit and three days to descend, though one suspects Norgay could have done better *without* the Europeans. In 2004, Pemba Dorji, another Sherpa, reached the peak in just 8 hours, 10 minutes.

MOUNT RUSHMORE

(America's greatest rock group)

USEFUL FOR: impressing your history teacher, nerdy dates, and South Dakotans

KEYWORDS: Rushmore, South Dakota, and the inevitable why?

THE FACT: Meet America's greatest rock group: George, Tom, Abe, and Teddy. But how exactly did this presidential summit come about? And more important, why South Dakota?

The fact is, a South Dakota state historian had a big idea in 1924: Turn a cliff in the Black Hills into a tribute to heroes of the Old West. And sculptor John Gutzon de la Mothe Borglum liked the idea, but not the choice of subjects. So the idea morphed a little, and a quartet of presidential busts was opened to the public in October 1941. Mount Rushmore, which cost about $1 million to build and is the largest American artwork ever created, attracts 2.7 million visitors a year—even though it was never finished. America got into World War II and funds ran dry. That's why Lincoln is missing an ear. Either that, or that's van Gogh up there.

instant personalities

Talk about a pant well taken, Flamenco dancer **JOSÉ GRECO** took out an insurance policy through Lloyd's of London against his trousers splitting during a performance.

Showing off his jujitsu abilities, poet **EZRA POUND** is well known for having flung poet Robert Frost over his shoulders.

As president, **GEORGE WASHINGTON** pulled in a salary of nearly $25k a year—roughly $1 million today. So it's no wonder he started living the high life immediately, buying leopard-skin robes for all his horses and spending seven percent of his income on alcohol.

NAPPING

(like a Movie Mogul)

USEFUL FOR: cocktail parties, business lunches, justifying lazing in the hammock when you're supposed to be out mowing the lawn

KEYWORDS: snooze, sleep, slumber, power naps, or Sam Goldwyn

THE FACT: Sam Goldwyn, one of Hollywood's most prominent film producers, believed in the power of working hard. He also believed in the power of a good afternoon's sleep.

It's no secret that Sam Goldwyn was a workaholic who demanded a lot from his employees. But like any good mogul, he also believed in pampering himself. Every day after lunch, Sam would take a siesta, disappearing into a room adjacent to his office, changing into pajamas, and sleeping for an hour. According to biographer Arthur Marx, Goldwyn—the man behind such classics as *Wuthering Heights* and *The Best Years of Our Lives*—believed a 60-minute afternoon nap was the secret to good health. One day he recommended the practice to two writers working on a script for a Danny Kaye picture. "You ought to try it, too," he said. Then, realizing that he didn't want the scribes sleeping on company time, he added, ". . . In your cases, eat a half-hour, sleep a half-hour."

NATIONAL ANTHEMS

(one that's easy to love, but hard to sing)

USEFUL FOR: Olympics, ball game banter, anytime someone fumbles the words to a song

KEYWORDS: Please rise for the national anthem

THE FACT: Every time you struggle a bit with "The Star Spangled Banner," just be glad that you're not from South Africa.

Like the nation itself, the South African National Anthem is a combination of words from several different ethnic groups. During the apartheid era, the white government had its anthem, *"Die Stem van Suid Afrika"* (The Call of South Africa). Of course, Nelson Mandela's African National Congress had its own separate-but-unofficial tune: *"Nkosi Sikelel' iAfrica"* (God Bless Africa). Then, when apartheid finally ended, and blacks and whites were legally forced to coexist, the two anthems were forced to coexist with equal status. That is, until 1995, when the pieces were melded to form the current national anthem in all its disjointed glory. Just how awkward is it? The anthem changes key in the middle, and is in *five* different languages. Starting as *"Nkosi,"* the tune goes on to sample the more prevalent of South Africa's many native languages. Verse 1 is in Xhosa. Verse 2, Zulu. Verse 3, Sesotho. Then the key switches and *"Die Stem"* powers through. Verse 4 is in Afrikaans, and verse 5 is in English. Whew!

NEW COKE, PART I

(the idea)

USEFUL FOR: cocktail parties, '80s nostalgia, and picking up people at the vending machine

KEYWORDS: the biggest mistake in history

THE FACT: In the early 1980s, the cola wars were in heavy combat, and Coke was dangerously close to losing its number-one spot to Pepsi. Its (poor) solution? A newly formulated version of the original soda.

On April 23, 1985, New Coke was released to the American public amid a barrage of media hype. The result was nothing short of a national crisis. Consumers were relentlessly enraged, comparing the taste of New Coke to "sewer water," "furniture polish," and worse, "two-day-old Pepsi." Before long, Old Coke had a thriving black market, with a case going for as much as $30. Other avid drinkers had supplies shipped to them from Canada or created stockpiles in their basements. But, apparently, you didn't even have to taste New Coke to be extremely angry about the beverage. The simple act of altering the formula at all set off its own firestorm. One disgusted consumer commented, "It's like spitting on the flag." Said one husband and father of two: "I couldn't have been more surprised if someone had told me that I was gay."

NEW COKE, PART II

(the damage done)

USEFUL FOR: telling people that whatever their mistake, it can't be *that* bad

KEYWORDS: hooray, hallelujah, or thank you, Jesus

THE FACT: In those first two months after New Coke hit the market the company received over 40,000 letters of complaint and 6,000 calls to its 800 number every day.

Only 87 days after its launch, the company reintroduced the original Coke formula as Coke Classic to subdue the masses. The return of Coke was considered so important to the American people that Peter Jennings of ABC News interrupted *General Hospital* to break the story on national TV. So what were the Coke execs thinking? Surprisingly, the launch of New Coke was based on the most exhaustive market research project in history. To the tune of $4 million, Coke conducted over 200,000 blind taste tests in which New Coke outperformed both Pepsi and Old Coke. Their mistake? Neglecting the emotional value of the soda to the American public.

NIETZSCHE

USEFUL FOR: academic gatherings, chatting with philosophers, and clearing Nietzsche's good name

KEYWORDS: superman, will to power, or Nietzsche

THE FACT: Seems like you've got to be pretty cocky to pen a phrase like "God is dead," but the famed philosopher Friedrich Nietzsche was more parts mild-mannered Emmanuel than anything else.

In fact, the bold, seemingly atheistic statement was actually a rail against the corruption of the church at the time. But the guy whose autobiographical *Ecce Homo* includes such chapters as "Why I Am So Wise," "Why I Am So Clever," and "Why I Write Such Good Books" was actually an unassuming man. His belief in "the will to power" as the most basic human drive finds little reflection in his own life outside his fantasies. Though he fancied himself a warrior and a ladies' man, Nietzsche's military service was brief and unspectacular, and he never had a lover. As a bad boy in college, he may have visited a brothel or two, though. One theory suggests that the insanity that cut his career short and institutionalized him for the last 11 years of his life was the result of untreated syphilis.

NIXON

(and the Beefeaters)

USEFUL FOR: cocktail parties, entertaining British guests, mocking anyone who remembers (or voted for) Richard Nixon

KEYWORDS: Nixon, Secret Service, presidential initiatives

THE FACT: Playing the role of fashion police at the White House, President Richard M. Nixon actually tried to makeover the Secret Service to look more like troops protecting a king.

Richard M. Nixon liked a bit of pomp (with occasional circumstance). After all, Tricky Dick often saw other heads of state protected by guards in bright-colored uniforms with shiny trim or tall fur hats (as in Britain's famous Beefeaters outside Queen Elizabeth's official London residence). But what did the White House have? Guys in dark, plain security uniforms. Wanting a piece of the regal action, Nixon ordered a redesign of the outfits worn by White House guards. Unveiled in 1970, the new duds featured gold-trimmed tunics and rigid, peaked hats reminiscent of 19th-century Prussia. The royalist look didn't go over so well with Americans. Critics howled. Comedians snickered. And the White House immediately threw out the Prussian hats. Within a few years the fancy duds (along with their chief proponent) were retired entirely.

NOUGAT

(and its mysterious origins)

USEFUL FOR: cocktail parties, grocery store lines, and impressing sweet tooths of all ages

KEYWORDS: Where does nougat come from?

THE FACT: Like falafel and the number 0, nougat is yet another product of Middle Eastern genius.

Originally made from a mixture of honey, nuts, and spices, the basic recipe for nougat was transplanted to Greece, where it lost the spices and gained the name "nugo." Later cultural exchanges brought the treat to France, where it became "nougat," and the recipe switched ground walnuts to ground almonds. In 1650, the French made another change for the better, adding beaten egg whites and creating the fluffier, modern nougat texture. The first commercial nougat factory opened in Montélimar, France, in the late 18th century, and today the area is renowned for its nougat, with about a dozen manufacturers producing the sugary treat. As for its ugly American cousin, the nougat you're probably familiar with from candy bars, it's not "true nougat." The imitation stuff is chewier, less almondy, and contains enough artificial preservatives to make a French candy maker wince.

NUTS

(isn't it time you met the betels?)

USEFUL FOR: cocktail parties, barroom banter, and chatting up people from South Asia

KEYWORDS: dip, chew, or Nicorette

THE FACT: The betel nut, which is actually the seed of a certain palm chewed with the leaf of a certain vine, is supposedly the third most popular recreational drug in the world (after alcohol and tobacco).

From India through Southeast Asia and well into the Pacific, this mild intoxicant is often the drug of choice. Chewing it makes the saliva flow freely while coloring it deeply; if you see gloppy masses of red spittle all over the sidewalks, you know that you are in betel country. In many tribal societies of Southeast Asia, betel is a cornerstone of sociability; sharing one's stash is how friendships are cemented and courtships initiated. Whether it's good for the teeth, however, is a matter of some debate.

OBJECTION!

(my attorney's asleep)

USEFUL FOR: cocktail parties, prison conversations, scaring defendants into paying for better lawyers

KEYWORDS: lawyer, incompetence, or attorney-cot privilege

THE FACT: Calvin Burdine was scheduled to die on April 11, 1995, 12 years after being convicted of killing his boyfriend in Houston. But a federal judge stopped the execution a few hours before it was scheduled.

What prompted the justice's change of heart? Well, amongst other things he was troubled that Burdine's lawyer had slept through portions of the trial. Amazingly, a three-member federal appeals court panel overruled the judge, reasoning that a defendant had no constitutional right to a conscious attorney (this was Texas, after all). Fortunately for Burdine, however, a full appeals court ordered a new trial, and the U.S. Supreme Court concurred. As of 2004, Burdine was doing life in a Texas prison after a plea bargain. And lawyers all over the country were trying to stay awake.

OPUS DEI

USEFUL FOR: chatting up atheists, conspiracy theorists, and people who just plain love Dan Brown

KEYWORDS: *The Da Vinci Code*, Catholic sects, and secret societies

THE FACT: The Catholic sect Opus Dei has a $42-million, 17-story building on Lexington Avenue in New York, claims 85,000 members in 60 countries, and it's just now surfacing on the pop culture radar screen.

Founded in 1928 by St. Josemariá Escrivá, Opus Dei is the short name for the Prelature for the Holy Cross and the Work of God. The sect stresses a return to traditional Catholic orthodoxy and behavior, especially celibacy, with members falling into one of three levels. Numeraries live in Opus Dei facilities, devote their time and money to the prelature, attend mass daily, and engage in mortification of the flesh (wearing a spiked chain around the thigh called a cilice, taking cold showers, or flagellating themselves). Next come Associates (kind of like Numeraries, but living "off campus"), then Supernumeraries (the rank-and-file members). Critics accuse the group of links to right-wing organizations, including Franco's fascist government in Spain, and of anti-Semitism and intolerance.

OSLO

*(and why the city screamed for **The Scream**)*

USEFUL FOR: museum dates, chatting up art lovers, and basically anytime you walk into a college dorm room

KEYWORDS: art heists, Munch (the name, not the verb) or munch (despite what we just said, you can use the verb to bring up the name to bring up the fact)

THE FACT: *The Scream*, Edvard Munch's 1893 expressionistic masterpiece of anxiety and despair, is one of the most famous paintings in the entire world. And on Sunday, August 22, 2004, administrators at Oslo's Munch Museum were definitely given reason to let life imitate the art.

In broad daylight, armed thieves yanked *The Scream* and another famous Munch, *Madonna*, off the wall, then made a break for it. Police found only the getaway car and two empty frames. Understandably, Norwegians reacted with disbelief and outrage at the theft of two national treasures. Oddly enough, this wasn't the first time the painting was purloined. There are actually *four* versions of *The Scream*. Another version was stolen in October 1994 from Oslo's National Gallery Art Museum. That one turned up three months later, but the most recently ripped off version remains missing.

OZONE

(and condoms?)

USEFUL FOR: cocktail parties, bachelor parties, and definitely, definitely office parties (spread the word!)

KEYWORDS: sex, photocopier, or sex on the photocopier

THE FACT: We think of ozone as a useful gas. And indeed it is, as long as it's up there in the stratosphere where it belongs. It's a little less helpful when it's messing about with your birth control.

Ozone forms when oxygen is exposed to ultraviolet light, and it's a good thing because ozone's a great absorber of ultraviolet radiation, thus protecting us from skin cancer. At ground level, however, ozone is a pollutant, forming as a result of internal combustion in our car engines. It's also the characteristic smell you sniff around photocopiers or other electrical devices. While ozone irritates our lungs, it can also affect our sex lives. Condoms are made of natural rubber, a substance that degrades on exposure to ozone. In layman's terms, this means that your protection needs protection if you're storing it around a photocopier.

PADDLE BALL

(Aztec style)

USEFUL FOR: half-time discussions, seventh-inning stretches, and after any call involving the roughing of a player

KEYWORDS: brutal, sports, man down, or just the word *ouch*

THE FACT: Playing ball, Aztec style, tended to get pretty rough, pretty quickly. Even worse? Losing meant sacrificing more than just your pride.

A ceremonial ball game played by the Aztecs a few hundred years before the European discovery of America, Ullamalitzli called for players on two teams to don large stone belts or hip paddles that were used to bounce a small rubber ball back and forth down a narrow court with inclined stone walls. The players used each other's bodies and the walls as they attempted to maneuver the ball into a small stone ring high above mid-court, an extremely difficult task. The game ended when either side scored a goal. Amazingly enough, the game enjoyed long popularity among the native peoples of Mexico and Central America before the Aztecs played it. Of course, the stakes were a little greater when the Aztecs came to play. In their version of the sport, at the end of the game one of the captains was sacrificed to the gods, giving even more meaning to the phrase "sore loser."

instant personalities

To make himself more attractive to the opposite sex, **SALVADOR DALI** used to shave his armpits and wear a homemade scent made of fish glue and cow manure.

As a child, the parents of famed poet **RAINER MARIA RILKE** dressed him up in girl's clothing and referred to him as Sophia.

For the three years he managed to scrape by, **WILLIAM FAULKNER** might have been one of the postal service's worst employees. Not only did he spend most of his days reading unclaimed periodicals on the job, but he also threw away most mail rather than sorting it.

PAGANINI

(sells his soul and fetches a good price)

USEFUL FOR: cocktail parties, classical music intermissions, and chatting up string players

KEYWORDS: Robert Johnson, Led Zeppelin, or any other big name person who supposedly sold his soul

THE FACT: Forget what you've heard about Robert Johnson and the crossroads, Niccolò Paganini was accused of selling his soul years before the blues was around.

It's true (the accusation part, at least!), Italian violinist and composer Niccolò Paganini was one of the most astounding virtuosos of all time. He had amazing technique and enormous passion. He also promoted himself shamelessly, doing tricks to astonish his audience. Often before a concert he would saw partway through three of the four strings on his violin. In performance, those three strings broke, forcing him to play an entire piece on one string. Rumors flew that Paganini had sold his soul to the devil in order to play so well. And sometimes Paganini would order the lights dimmed while he played particularly spooky music. Everybody fainted—when the candles were lit again, the room appeared to be full of dead bodies sprawled everywhere. (Clearly, it didn't take much to stun an audience in those days.)

THE PAPER CLIP

(fighting Nazis since World War II)

USEFUL FOR: water cooler conversation, making friends at Kinko's, Staples, or OfficeMax

KEYWORDS: Norway, pride, Nazis, or office supplies

THE FACT: In 1899, soon to be Norwegian icon Johan Vaaler designed a paper clip and promptly set out to get his idea patented. He quickly found out that Norway had no patent laws to speak of.

Undeterred by his countrymen's apparent lack of creativity (or, at least, foresight), the tenacious Norwegian obtained a copyright in Germany and, later, another in America. Interestingly, Norway has yet to recover from the excitement surrounding this achievement. Far from a simple office supply, residents consider the paper clip a symbol of national pride—like the eagle in America, only less endangered. During World War II, the occupying Nazi forces made it illegal for Norwegians to wear or display images of their former king, so resistance fighters looked for a more subtle way to display their sympathies. A paper clip fastened to the lapel proved just the thing, and it soon came to represent a free Norway.

PASSENGER PIGEONS

(and one terrible 14-year-old)

USEFUL FOR: PTA meetings, chatting up bird lovers, convincing yourself your teen would never do that

KEYWORDS: hunting, conservation, or extinction

THE FACT: If you're hankering for a peek at the passenger pigeon, you're flat out of luck. Oh, and you can thank a 14-year-old kid for your disappointment.

The naturalist John James Audubon once reported seeing a flock of passenger pigeons so numerous it took three days to fly over them. And he wasn't exaggerating! In the early part of the 19th century, the birds were estimated to make up as much as 40 percent of North America's entire avian population. But the abundance of the creatures made them easy marks. Effortlessly hunted, the birds were mowed down mostly for food but occasionally for sport, with some "sportsmen" bagging as many as 5,000 in a day. Unfortunately, the birds were unable to sustain themselves except in large flocks, and they quickly dwindled. In 1900, a 14-year-old boy shot the last wild passenger pigeon out of existence. (Boys *will* be boys.) Fourteen years later, the last one in captivity died at the Cincinnati Zoo. Her name was Martha.

PATERNITY

(and some painful traditions)

USEFUL FOR: barroom banter, letting people in the waiting room know just how good they have it

KEYWORDS: dad, daddy, pop, or stud

THE FACT: According to some traditions in French Guyana, several days before his wife is expected to give birth, the husband is expected to quit working.

In fact, he's also expected to maintain a strict diet, because many foods consumed by the father are believed to directly affect the unborn child. When the baby finally arrives, the woman must return to work as soon as she is able. The father, however, is restricted to his bed and kept in relative seclusion. After about six weeks of this, relatives cut openings in his skin and rub his body with a ground pepper plant. (If only he could just buy a few cigars.) Similar ceremonies are found in remote areas all over the world, and they are all related to the concept of couvade, in which the father is expected to share in the pain of his wife's birthing experience. These days, when expectant fathers experience "sympathy pains" in the abdomen, it's known as "couvade syndrome."

PERFUME

(and why Willy can stop worrying)

USEFUL FOR: perfume counter conversation, chatting up someone from PETA, and calming down your pet whale

KEYWORDS: ambergris, cologne, or whaling

THE FACT: Whales can finally relax! Today's chemists have learned how to mimic ambergris in the laboratory, causing high-pitched sighs of relief in oceans across the world.

For those of you unaware, ambergris is the waxy liquid coating the stomachs of sperm whales, and it protects them from the sharp bones of the cuttlefish they eat. When fresh, it's soft and black and smells awful. When exposed to sun and water, it hardens, becomes lighter colored, and develops a pleasant smell. Bizarrely, ambergris is an excellent "fixative" that keeps perfume's scent from evaporating too quickly and for this reason was once a prize booty for whalers. A piece of ambergris weighing 922 pounds was once found floating in the ocean, making its discoverer instantly wealthy. But synthetic analogues have now eliminated the need to kill whales for perfume manufacturing. And ladies no longer have to cope with the notion of anointing themselves with whale regurgitation.

PET ROCKS

USEFUL FOR: cheap gift nostalgia, convincing your kids they're spoiled for having a dog

KEYWORDS: boulder, stone, or Lassie

THE FACT: Pet rocks were perhaps the greatest idea P. T. Barnum never had, and there were more than a few suckers born for it every minute.

The brilliant mind behind this moronic craze is Gary Dahl, a California advertising exec. Gary conceived the idea one evening in 1975 while sitting around at a bar with his buddies pontificating about the hassles of owning a pet and jokingly proposing rocks as the perfect low-maintenance pal. Still amused by the idea the next morning, or still drunk, Dahl decided to create a prototype, complete with carrying case and the *Pet Rock Training Manual*. In August of that year, he took the kit with him to the annual gift show, then in New York, where Neiman Marcus (of all stores) immediately snatched up 500 of them. By the end of October, Dahl was shipping 10,000 pet rocks out every day. By the end of the 1975 Christmas season, he had used up three tons of stone from Rosarita Beach in Baja, Mexico, and made several million dollars. So when the pet fad quickly waned in early 1976, he had man's second best friend—a fat stack of bills—to keep him smiling.

PETS

(you probably shouldn't let around your kids)

USEFUL FOR: barroom banter, making small talk at the Reptile House, and deciding what pet Santa shouldn't get little Timmy

KEYWORDS: cold-blooded, lizard, or the worst pet ever

THE FACT: Among morbid options, if your choice is between dying alone in a house full of cats, or dying alone in a house full of monitor lizards, we suggest you choose the former.

Although highly intelligent creatures, monitor lizards are notoriously unaffectionate (at least toward our species), and more than a little temperamental when it comes to handling. In fact, careless owners are frequently subject to tail lashings and toothy "love" bites. And as appealing as that sounds, before you rush off to get yourself a pet monitor you might want to consider the tale of Newark, Delaware's Ronald Huff. After Huff passed away in his efficiency apartment, his seven hungry pals (clearly not in mourning) made a buffet of his body.

PEZ

(now in delicious flower flavors?)

USEFUL FOR: stirring up some conversation anytime you see a PEZ dispenser

KEYWORDS: azalea, daffodil, or pansy

THE FACT: No, those aren't typos. Although it would be equally disgusting, we're talking about *flower*, not flour.

Introduced in the late 1960s, flower-flavored PEZ was designed to appeal to the hippie generation, complete with groovy, mod packaging. But even in the decade full of free love, no love could be found for the flavor power of the flower. Floral scents make for great perfume, but nobody eats perfume, and apparently, there's a reason why. The flower version flopped, and became the next addition to PEZ's long and disturbing list of flavor failures. Since its introduction in 1927, the company has also sold (however briefly) coffee, licorice, eucalyptus, menthol, and cinnamon flavors.

PHYSICISTS

(as in the one you definitely want at your party)

USEFUL FOR: cocktail parties, impressing nerdy dates, and anytime you're arguing who's the greatest physicist of all time

KEYWORDS: atom bomb, safecracking, or physics

THE FACT: Anyone whose hobbies include bongo playing, chasing skirts, and picking government locks can't be your typical physicist—and Richard Feynman certainly wasn't!

One of the most famous physicists of the post–World War II era, Feynman contributed heavily to the Manhattan Project, garnered a Nobel Prize for his work in quantum electrodynamics, and contributed key insights on the presidential team investigating the NASA *Challenger* disaster. He was also well known for banging away on his bongos whenever he got the chance and for trying to perfect the art of picking up women (from college parties to red light districts). If you'd like some insight into his mischievous personality, though, consider how he let the great minds working on the Manhattan Project know that their "classified documents" weren't exactly safe. Feynman studied up a bit on safecracking, then picked the government locks with ease, taking nothing from the vaults. Instead, he left amusing notes for the officials letting them know just how good their security was.

POLO
(with a dead goat!)

USEFUL FOR: impressing your gym teacher, disturbing folks at the polo grounds, and chatting up anyone with a hatred for goats

KEYWORDS: goats, polo, or Afghani X games

THE FACT: While snobby English aristocrats and that guy on those Ralph Lauren shirts usually play the sport with a small ball, we think they should be using a human head or a dead goat. After all, that is how the "sport of kings" began.

Over a thousands of years ago polo was played under a different name: "bughazi." In fact, the game wasn't so much a leisure activity as military training for Persian cavalry, and it was possibly adopted from tribesmen in modern-day Pakistan or Afghanistan. Besides the dead goat, there were other differences in play. Instead of four players on a side, the ancient version involved armies of men—literally—with hundreds or even thousands of players on each side. It's believed that the first tournament was won by Turkish tribesmen playing against the Persians in 600 BCE. And although the game was often played with animal heads, the Mongol conqueror Genghis Khan made a popular change, instituting the practice of decapitating military opponents and making a game ball of their noggins, still in their helmets.

PONZI SCHEME

USEFUL FOR: cocktail parties, impressing your history teacher, and making quick decisions on all those son-of-a-wealthy Nigerian forwards

KEYWORDS: scam, scheme, cheat, or dupe

THE FACT: Being a scam artist is bad enough, but having a type of scam named after you is a perverse sort of immortality.

Consider the case of Charles Ponzi, who showed great chutzpah even by 1920s standards. Promising investors a return rate of 100 percent in just 90 days, Ponzi lured trusting thousands into his Security and Exchange Company (no relation to the Securities and Exchange Commission, which regulates U.S. financial markets). But the supposed whiz kid merely used the new funds to pay off existing investors, a practice now known as a Ponzi scheme. The arrangement collapsed when the authorities began investigating, and after doing a stint in the slammer, "the Ponz" finally got a real job, working for Alitalia, the Italian national airline.

POPCORN

(and its devilish origins)

USEFUL FOR: impressing your history and science teachers, and convincing your ultra-religious relatives not to steal from your buttery tub

KEYWORDS: popcorn, extra butter, Pop Secret

THE FACT: If you want to know why the devil popcorn tastes so darn good, chief Quadequina has a pretty original answer for you.

English colonists were introduced to popcorn at the first Thanksgiving in Plymouth by Quadequina, a Native American chief. They were told that popcorn pops because a demon living inside each kernel gets angry and has to escape when placed near heat. If you're looking for a better explanation, look to the steam. Each kernel of corn has a small amount of moisture inside that changes to steam when heated. Gases expand as the temperature increases so that pressure builds up inside the kernel until it can take it no more. Then there's a sudden explosion, and the kernel is literally blown inside out. Interestingly enough, if a small hole is bored into an unpopped kernel it won't pop because the steam has a means of escaping.

POPES

(gone wild)

USEFUL FOR: cocktail parties, confession booths, and shocking Mother Superior

KEYWORDS: bad popes, dying in the act, or bad popes dying in the act

THE FACT: Sometimes religious power corrupts, and absolute religious power corrupts absolutely—well, at least in the case of some of history's worst popes. Believe it or not, history caught more than a few of these pontiffs with their holy pants down.

That's right, we're talking about popes, plural. Apparently papal infallibility only gets you so far. First, we have Pope Leo VII (d. 939 CE), who died of a heart attack during sex. Then there's Pope John XII (d. 963 CE), who was reportedly bludgeoned to death, naked in bed, by the jealous husband of his mistress. And who could forget Pope John XIII (d. 972 CE), who, remarkably enough, departed this earthly existence in exactly the same way as John XII. Then, of course, there's good ol' Pope Paul II (d. 1471 CE), who for variety's sake had a heart attack while getting it on with a page boy.

PORN

(of the panda variety)

USEFUL FOR: barroom banter, bachelor party planning, and chatting up your date at the zoo

KEYWORDS: Ling-Ling, Hsing-Hsing, and Ralph (the Panda)

THE FACT: We don't want to pass judgment about their "performance" in the wild, but while in captivity, male giant pandas have a very hard time finding (or keeping) their mojo. Guess what helps them get their groove on.

Basically, the mojo dilemma has forced scientists to try a series of different methods to help put pandas in the mood. In the mid-1990s, researchers in Shanghai tried out a few Chinese medications thought to increase sex drive. They succeeded in raising the male libido, but simultaneously raised their tempers, making females the subject of more violence than romance. In 2002, scientists tried a heaping helping of the erectile dysfunction medicine Viagra, but that didn't work either. So what's the most successful aphrodisiac so far? Panda porn! For several hours a day during mating season, researchers in China played X-rated video of pandas having sex for their subjects and reported increased rates of arousal.

instant personalities

Folk singer/songwriter and country boy **JOHN DENVER** once got so angry at his wife, Annie, that he sawed his bed in half.

Besides his many hunting and sporting accidents, **ERNEST HEMINGWAY** was notorious for wrecking a number of planes. During an African safari in 1954, he crashed near Murchison Falls. Within forty-eight hours, he'd crashed again in a second plane.

When drummer **KEITH MOON** was asked by a hotel manager to keep the noise down on his 21st birthday, he threw a fit. He also threw a cake right at the manager. He then proceeded to streak, steal a fire extinguisher, wreck his room, dive into the pool, trip on a doorsill, and, finally, knock out a front tooth. Holiday Inn promptly banned him for the rest of his life.

PORT ROYAL

(the sin-iest place on earth!)

USEFUL FOR: barroom banter, bachelor party planning, and impressing any happy-go-lucky buccaneers you run into

KEYWORDS: sin city, pirates, or "what happens in Vegas . . ."

THE FACT: For all its debauchery, Vegas still can't hold a candle to the original capital of British Jamaica, Port Royal, a.k.a. the most sin-sational place on earth!

It's true: The area was a hotbed for pirates and Limey officials who were happy to look the other way—for a piece of the action. When pirate crews rolled into town they could enjoy a wide array of vice, including prostitutes, gambling, liquor, and drugs smuggled from the Orient and the Middle East. If that doesn't sound like enough fun for you, the streets literally echoed with the sounds of sin: from ruckus brawls to the incessant nursery rhyme "Sing a Song of Sixpence." And just to prove how corrupt it was, Henry Morgan, an infamous pirate admiral, was actually made lieutenant governor of the Port in 1674. Of course, such dens of sin can't last forever, and Port Royal was destroyed in 1692 by an earthquake that dropped three quarters of it into the sea. It seemed someone upstairs had a cross to bear against this humble burg.

PREGNANCY

(and the car-pool lane)

USEFUL FOR: cocktail parties, making friends at Lamaze class, and bringing up anytime you're stuck in traffic

KEYWORDS: knocked up, HOV lane, or traffic cop

THE FACT: Can a pregnant woman drive in the car-pool lane? Expectant mothers, start your engines!

In 1987, a pregnant California woman was ticketed for driving "by herself" in the car-pool lane. Sure, the citation was only for $52, but she sued anyway, contending that her five-month-old fetus constituted a second person. Lo and behold, the jury agreed with her, despite the prosecution's argument that women could then just stuff pillows up their dresses to drive "car-pool" on California's freeways. But, as it turns out, the California Highway Patrol took care of that concern, brushing off the case as a bunch of hooey. Verdict or not, officers said, they would continue to ticket solo drivers, even if they claimed to be pregnant.

PRESIDENTIAL AFFAIRS

(and good old Grover Cleveland)

USEFUL FOR: election seasons, impressing your fourth-grade history teacher, and defending Grover Cleveland's reputation

KEYWORDS: Presidential affairs, scandals, or dillydallying

THE FACT: In 1873, a young, politically aspiring bachelor named Grover Cleveland met Maria Halpin, a 35-year-old widow with two children. Apparently, he more than just liked her.

Maria's looks and personality made her the talk of Buffalo and Grover soon found himself among Halpin's many suitors. Well, more than just a suitor. In 1874, Halpin bore a son and insinuated that old Grover was the pop. Grover, not intending to marry Maria, decided to do the right thing and bear financial responsibility for the child. During the 1884 presidential campaign, however, Cleveland's opposition dug up the old story and printed it in the press. A number of clergy members supporting Cleveland did a study of the case and found that after the "preliminary offense" Cleveland had done the honorable thing. More important in their minds, he'd shielded many married men in Buffalo (and their families) from public scandal. Because of this, even many of Grover's opponents supported his run for the presidency.

PYGMY

(in a zoo?)

USEFUL FOR: barroom banter, impressing your history teacher, and shocking anyone fond of zoos

KEYWORDS: pygmy, World's Fair, or the Bronx

THE FACT: In 1906, thousands of curious people were rushing to the Bronx Zoo in New York to see its newest and most "exotic" exhibit: a 4-foot, 11-inch African pygmy.

The tragically exploited man, named Ota Benga, was a member of the Mbuti peoople of Zaire. Explorer Samuel Verner purchased him at a slave market to put him on display in the 1904 St. Louis World's Fair. After, Ota Benga returned to Zaire, only to be rejected for being tainted by the white man. Verner brought Ota back, and presented him to the eccentric director of the Bronz Zoo, William T. Hornaday, who gladly agreed to "care for" him. Ota Benga was locked in the zoo's monkey house and put on display with a few chimpanzees, a gorilla, and an orangutan as "ancient ancestors of man." The exhibit rightfully sparked a wave of controversy from the African-American community and (interestingly) churchmen, who feared Ota Benga would convince people of Darwin's theory of evolution. Fortunately, the pressure from such groups eventually forced Hornaday to release him.

THE QUADRO

(the littlest big fake)

USEFUL FOR: cocktail parties, barroom banter, and supporting that whole "sucker born every minute" argument

KEYWORDS: fake, fraud, or *The Music Man*

THE FACT: The Quadro Corporation of Harleyville, South Carolina, had an impressive client list: public schools, police agencies, the U.S. Customs office, and Inspector General's office to name a few. But no one quite knows why.

The product they sold was the top-of-the-line Quadro QRS 250G (also known as the Quadro Tracker, available for $1,000), and the company boasted its ability to find drugs, weapons, or virtually anything worth looking for. The small plastic box supposedly contained frequency chips of an advanced sort not known to "regular" science. Driven by static electricity, the Quadro would resonate at exactly the same frequency as the searched-for item. When the FBI opened the box, however, they found nothing inside. Quadro threatened to sue Sandia Laboratories when Sandia suggested that the device was fraudulent, but eventually Quadro became the bigger company and just closed its doors.

QUOTES

(and the guy who loved compiling them)

USEFUL FOR: academic gatherings, impressing nerdy dates and people who love forwards

KEYWORDS: *Bartlett's Familiar Quotations*

THE FACT: As anyone who's worked retail can attest to, there's often a lot of downtime, and John Bartlett no doubt experienced plenty while working at the Harvard University bookstore.

But instead of gluing the pages of popular books together or locking coworkers in the lavatory, Bartlett spent his downtime compiling his book of *Familiar Quotations*, which was first printed in 1855. Filled with quotes from literature as ancient as the Old Testament and as quirky as the "Annals of Sporting," Bartlett once said about them, "I have gathered a posie of other men's flowers, and nothing but the thread that binds them is mine own." Throughout the continued success of his book (and subsequent editions), Bartlett joined the publishing firm of Little, Brown and Company in 1863 and became senior partner in 1878, where he never uttered the phrase "gathered a posie of other men's flowers" ever again.

RATS

(in the courtroom)

USEFUL FOR: cocktail parties, making headway with a judge, and clearing the awkward silence after someone's just told a lawyer joke

KEYWORDS: rats, courtroom, really bad excuses

THE FACT: Believe it or not, there was a time in European history when people actually used to take animals to court. In this case, the rats actually managed to land themselves an amazing attorney.

When the French province of Autun's barley began disappearing, the local rats were charged with stealing. When they failed to answer a summons (yes, really!), their appointed lawyer, Bartholomew Chassenée, argued that a single summons was invalid because the rats lived in different villages. New summonses were issued. This time Chassenée argued some of his clients were aged and infirm and needed more time. After that, he argued the rats were afraid to come to court because of all the cats along the way. When villagers refused to obey a court order to lock up their cats, charges against the rodents were dismissed. Chassenée later became France's leading jurist. As for the dirty rats, they presumably returned to lives of crime.

REVENGE

(and one of the most one-sided battles of all time)

USEFUL FOR: half-time shows, ballparks, and anytime you're watching a team get slaughtered

KEYWORDS: outmatch, crush, kill, bloodbath, or not really fair—even for love and war

THE FACT: When the forces of British general Charles Gordon were surrounded and eventually destroyed by Islamic fundamentalist tribesmen at Khartoum, Sudan, in 1885, the blow to British prestige was tremendous. In fact, the British quickly decided not to get humiliated again.

The imperialist nation was so embarrassed that it decided the event demanded a total and overwhelming response. To get revenge, the British shipped a well-trained army to fight the native Muslim rebels in central Sudan. But the army wasn't just well trained, they were well armed and were even carrying Gatling guns—prototype machine guns that drew ammunition from a long straight clip filing through the firing chamber. The result at the battle of Omdurman in 1898 was decisive and horrendous, resulting in the slaughter of tens of thousands of native tribesmen with virtually no British casualties.

RICHARD III

(and Shakespeare's knack for exaggerating)

USEFUL FOR: cocktail parties, academic gatherings, and making small talk during Shakespeare intermissions

KEYWORDS: hunchback, Richard III, or bad PR

THE FACT: Despite what everybody thinks, Richard III probably was *not* a hunchback. So why'd old Will Shakespeare depict him that way?

To thrive as a playwright, Shakespeare needed to stay on the good side of his monarch, Elizabeth I. And since Queen Bess's grandfather, Henry VII, had become king by defeating Richard III in battle, the queen had a family interest—and a personal stake—in seeing Richard remain a villain. Elizabeth's father, Henry VIII, had previously commissioned a biography of Richard in which he was portrayed as physically and morally misshapen, and Shakespeare stuck to the script. Given the playwright's skill, is it any wonder that the dramatic character of a hunchbacked bad guy caught on? Yet portraits painted during Richard's lifetime showed no pronounced deformity.

ROCK PAPER SCISSORS

USEFUL FOR: cocktail parties, chatting about extreme sports, and impressing everyone at recess

KEYWORDS: rock, paper, or scissors

THE FACT: From the playground to the annual RPS International World Championship (really, people, we're not kidding), outwitting your opponent is job number one for serious competitors. Not getting injured from playing might be number two.

According to the World RPS Society, one way to guess what hand someone will throw out is to know how many rounds they've won so far. Players who are in the lead will often use Scissors, because it's believed to symbolize aggression, while Paper is used for a more subtle attack. Rock is usually a last resort, when players feel their strategies are failing. There are also techniques you can use to mask your move, such as cloaking, in which players will pretend to throw Rock and then stick out two fingers at the last second to make Scissors. But if you're gonna play, be prepared to pay. In the late 1980s, Kenyan Mustafa Nwenge lost a match *and* the use of a finger when an overzealous opponent "cut his Paper" a little too zealously and crushed Nwenge's finger ligaments. So what is it that beats hospital bill? Not playing with morons.

ROGET

(the name on your thesaurus)

USEFUL FOR: cocktail parties, academic gathers, and anytime you're handing someone a thesaurus

KEYWORDS: what's another word for . . .

THE FACT: You know his last name from the spine of your desk reference set, but did you know Peter Mark Roget was the Doogie Howser of the 1800s?

By the age of 14, he was studying medicine at Edinburgh University in Scotland, and in his spare time, compiling a well-indexed catalog of fancy words that he used to enhance his medical and theoretical papers. In one such paper, the young brainiac (see also *egghead, smarty-pants, Poindexter*) described the optical illusion one witnessed when viewing a moving carriage through the blinds of a window, explaining the eye's ability to fill in the missing frames. It was groundbreaking research that would later lead to the invention of motion pictures. Of course, it would be decades until such technology was available, so Roget had to fall back on that book of words he'd been keeping. Fortunately, that worked out pretty well for him, and *Roget's Thesaurus* was born (i.e. sprouted, emerged, germinated).

ROLLER COASTERS, PART I

USEFUL FOR: cocktail parties, Sunday school, and making conversation in really long lines at Six Flags

KEYWORDS: you must be this tall . . .

THE FACT: When Coney Island became overrun with beer halls, LaMarcus Thompson, a preacher, feared the demon liquor would send the souls of the beachgoers straight to hell, so he decided to give them something else to scream about.

In 1884, Thompson shelled out $1,600 to open the Gravity Pleasure Switchback Railway, an incredibly lame ride that maxed out somewhere in the neighborhood of 6 miles per hour. Nevertheless, it was an instant hit with easily entertained Victorians. Even at a mere five cents a ticket, Thompson regained his investment in less than three weeks. As the money rolled in, he gave up preaching anything but the gospel of roller coasters and went on to become the original coaster tycoon.

ROLLER COASTERS, PART II

USEFUL FOR: cocktail parties, chatting up thrill seekers, and explaining to your kid why the coaster you just waited in line for 45 minutes to ride really was fast enough

KEYWORDS: Can't this thing go any faster?

THE FACT: Not all early roller coasters were as dull as Coney Island's first coaster, the Gravity Pleasure (which went a whopping 6 miles per hour). Of course, they weren't as safe, either.

In about 1895, a ride called the Flip-Flap Railway opened on Coney Island. It was arguably the world's first loop-the-loop-style coaster, but with one key difference: The loops of the Flip-Flap were perfect circles. This doesn't sound like a big problem . . . until you start considering physics. Modern coasters use elliptical loops and reach a maximum g-force of 6g's. By contrast, in the tight circles of the Flip-Flap, passengers experienced up to 12g's of gravitational force, which, coincidentally, is also the limit of force the human body can withstand. Many riders' necks were snapped as they hung on for dear life to safety-belt-less wooden carts. Despite this hazard, the death coaster managed to remain open for eight years.

instant personalities

"Peanuts" creator **CHARLES M. SCHULZ** hated getting his hair clipped at his pop's barbershop as a kid, because whenever "real" customers came in, he'd have to get up and walk around with only half a haircut. (Good grief!)

SIR ISAAC NEWTON only made one recorded comment during his term as a member of British Parliament: He asked that someone open the window.

By age 13 **THELONIOUS MONK** was so accomplished on the keys that the Apollo Theater banned him from the weekly amateur contest because he'd won too many times.

RONALD McDONALD

(secret agent man)

USEFUL FOR: barroom banter, drive-thru chatter, and anytime you spot a clown

KEYWORDS: top secret, covert ops, or Happy Meal

THE FACT: Who knew the CIA and McDonald's had so much in common?

McDonald's execs, like their less delicious counterparts at the Central Intelligence Agency, uphold an intense policy of employee secrecy. Clowns who portray Ronald McDonald are strictly forbidden to disclose their identities. It's also taboo for two (costumed) Ronalds to be in the same place at the same time. In fact, the only time they get together is at the biennial Ronald McDonald Convention, which, as you might imagine, is also very top secret. All of this helps maintain the image that Ronald, the second-most-recognizable figure worldwide (after Santa), is a single, magical character. There are, of course, many Ronalds—an estimated 250, in fact. Their average income is about $40,000 a year, but the busiest clowns can bring in as much as $100,000. The Ronald McDonald who appears in the company's television commercials earns a salary of more than $300,000. We could tell you who he is, but we'd be risking a lifetime of toyless Happy Meals. Some things just aren't worth the risk.

SADDAM

(and his sweet tooth)

USEFUL FOR: cocktail parties, chatting with Desert Storm vets, and making people really curious about one of the world's worst tyrants

KEYWORDS: Saddam Hussein, chocolate, pizza party menu

THE FACT: The bizarre contents of Saddam Hussein's residences—velvet paintings of Elvis and all—have provided endless fodder for cocktail conversations, but none like his fridge.

Amid the revelations of Saddam's incredibly bad taste, it also revealed that Saddam was a bit of a sugar fiend. In his last rather ignoble residence—the "spider hole" where he was finally apprehended in Ad Dawr in December 2003—American soldiers found a refrigerator filled with Mars and Bounty candy bars and 7-Up. Thank God! No longer relegated to the realm of middle school sleepovers and Little League pizza parties, these snack foods have finally broken through to a new demographic: dictators evading prosecution for crimes against humanity.

THE SAFETY PIN

USEFUL FOR: chatting with punks, moms who use natural diapers, and anyone who loves safety

KEYWORDS: pin, prick, or pinprick

THE FACT: If you're looking for someone to thank for the invention of the safety pin, all credit should go to Walter Hunt—and his inability to pay off his debts.

In 1849, Hunt was a prolific, if not entirely well off, inventor whose previous efforts included a repeating rifle, artificial stone, and an ice plow. Unable to draw any of his inventions, he was forced to hire a draftsman to produce the diagrams that had to be submitted with his patent applications. Several patents later, Hunt found himself in debt to the artist for a whopping $15. Realizing he wasn't going to get the cash, the draftsman proposed an alternate way for Hunt to pay him back. He dared Hunt to invent something using only a piece of wire and to hand over the rights. In return, the debt would be forgiven and the draftsman would pay Hunt $400. It seemed like a great deal—that is, until Hunt's hours of twisting produced the first practical safety pin. The draftsman walked away with a million-dollar patent under his belt, while Hunt got $400 and, we assume, a lifetime of bitterness.

SALIVA

(that'll get you tanked!)

USEFUL FOR: cocktail parties, barroom banter, and knowing what beverage not to order in the South Pacific

KEYWORDS: alcohol, drool, or what could possibly be worse than licking a toad to get a buzz

THE FACT: In much of the South Pacific, kava is the traditional drug of choice. Kava supposedly reduces inhibitions and enhances conviviality, much like alcohol. However, it isn't the drug itself so much as the traditional mode of preparation that often dismays outsiders.

The active substance in kava is apparently released in interaction with chemicals contained in human saliva. Kava roots are thus thoroughly chewed, the masticated mass is wrung out in a twisted cloth, and the resulting liquid is then ready for drinking. Even though young people with good teeth and fresh breath are usually the designated chewers, kava drinking is still likely to put off the fastidious traveler.

SCHOPENHAUER

(the poodle-loving pessimist)

USEFUL FOR: cocktail parties and talking about philosophy, without actually talking about philosophy

KEYWORDS: Schopenhauer, misogynist, or glass half empty

THE FACT: One of philosophy's most notorious sourpusses, Arthur Schopenhauer was a definite pessimist, and viewed reality as a malicious trap. In fact, he believed we live in the worst of all possible worlds.

As if that wasn't bad enough, though, notorious misogynist Schopenhauer once pushed a woman down a flight of stairs. Grudgingly, he paid her regular restitution for her injuries until her death, when he recorded in his journal, "The old woman dies, the burden is lifted." Schopenhauer despised noise but inexplicably had a fondness for something more odious—poodles. A series of disposable poodles were his constant companions for most of his life. Not a pleasant academic colleague, Schopenhauer resented the success of Hegel, whose philosophy he thought was the worst kind of nonsense. Perhaps planning to undo Hegel, Schopenhauer scheduled his course lectures at the same time as Hegel's. The result, however, was an early retirement for Arthur.

SCOPES (MONKEY) TRIAL

USEFUL FOR: PTA meetings, impressing your high school history teacher, and irritating people at Sunday school

KEYWORDS: creationism, evolution, biology class, or monkeys

THE FACT: Everyone knows the Monkey Trial had something to do with teaching evolution in school. Not everyone remembers the actual outcome, or the monkey that was made of the prosecution.

It was a simple case. A Dayton, Tennessee, teacher had taught Darwin's theory of evolution, in defiance of a new state law. But the charges quickly became international news when Clarence Darrow, the era's most famous liberal lawyer, took up teacher John Scopes's defense. The case only got more intriguing when William Jennings Bryan, the three-time presidential candidate, joined the prosecution. During the defense's case, Darrow stunned the courtroom by calling Bryan to the stand. For two hours, the two dueled over Bryan's literal interpretation of the Bible which hardly helped Mr. Scopes. Scopes was found guilty and fined $100. Bryan died a few days after the trial. But the state's ban on teaching evolution was reversed in 1967.

SEA MONKEYS

USEFUL FOR: cocktail parties, stirring up '60s nostalgia, and taking the wind out of an eight-year-old's sail

KEYWORDS: monkeys, brine shrimp, or the worst pet ever

THE FACT: Ah, sea monkeys. You know 'em; you love 'em; you're totally confused by 'em. Well, consider the monkey mystery solved.

Turns out, they're *Artemia salinas*, or brine shrimp. In the 1960s, inventor Harold von Braunhut discovered that the shrimp's eggs lie dormant in salt flats waiting for the right conditions before they spring to life, so he started experimenting with them for his toy product, Instant-Life. Later, he changed the name (and struck pop culture gold) after a colleague heard him call the creatures his "cute little sea monkeys." The shrimp became popular because of their ability to "come back to life" after being stored dry on a shelf, but fell from favor after children discovered that they had a lifespan of about a month. Over the years, however, von Braunhut managed to breed better sea monkeys—the shrimp can now live up to two years. As for von Braunhut, who passed away in 2003, he was also responsible for X-Ray Specs and the late-1980s hermit crab craze.

SHAKERS

USEFUL FOR: cocktail parties, barroom banter, anywhere martinis are being drunk

KEYWORDS: Shaker?

THE FACT: Officially known as the United Society of Believers in Christ's Second Appearing, the Shakers were founded in Manchester, England, in 1747. Nearly 250 years later, though, there isn't a whole lot of Shaking going on.

As a group of dissenting Quakers under the charismatic leadership of "Mother Ann" Lee, the Shakers came to America in 1774. Like most reform movements of the time, the Shakers were agriculturally based, and believed in common ownership of all property. Unlike most of the other groups, however, the Shakers practiced celibacy, including rejection of marital sex. So how exactly did the movement spread? Membership came via conversion or by the adoption of children. Shaker families consisted of "brothers" and "sisters" who lived in gender-segregated communal homes. And during the required Sunday community meetings it wasn't uncommon for members to break into a spontaneous dance, thus giving them the "shaker" label. However, their religious movement wasn't built to last. In fact, of the original 19 communities, there is only one in existence today.

SHAKESPEARE

(as in the whole typing monkeys thing)

USEFUL FOR: cocktail parties, dates at the zoo, and whenever someone brings up the idea of infinity

KEYWORDS: Shakespeare, monkeys, and typing

THE FACT: If a million monkeys typed on a million typewriters for a million years, would they produce a work of Shakespeare by chance? Well, not according to this experiment.

This notion has been used to indicate how over the vastness of time complex creations may arise from chance. Well, researchers at Plymouth University in England have carried out a small-scale experiment by placing a computer in an enclosure with six macaques (short-tailed monkeys). After pounding on it with a rock, defecating on it, and urinating on it, some of the monkeys did hit a few keystrokes, producing mostly a lot of S's. Theoretically, the hypothesis defies statistics. The odds of striking the correct sequence is so small that you'd have to have a million monkeys typing at a rate of 31,000,000 strokes a year (1 per second) each for a million years, and then multiply that amount by itself almost 200 times. We think there are better odds at winning the Powerball jackpot.

SHEEP

(specifically, the blackest one of the Brontë family)

USEFUL FOR: cocktail parties, impressing your English teacher, and making friends at the library (please keep the facts to a whisper)

KEYWORDS: *Wuthering Heights, Jane Eyre,* or any Brontë

THE FACT: Anne Brontë may have had an inferiority complex living with sisters like Charlotte and Emily, but she was hardly the least-accomplished child in the family.

That honor goes to their only brother, Branwell. As a child, Branwell showed a lot of promise as an artist and writer, and because of that, ironically enough, Branwell was considered the prodigy of the family. With high expectations, his parents sent him to attend the Royal Academy Schools in London, but that proved to be an embarrassing mistake. Pretty much all Branwell did while he was away was spend exorbitant amounts of family money, become a raging alcoholic and opium addict, sleep around with legions of different women, and get fired from jobs for not showing up or, in one case, "fiddling with the books."

SIBLING RIVALRY

USEFUL FOR: cocktail parties, chatting up the French, and consoling the Jan Brady in your family

KEYWORDS: Fredo Corleone, Jan Brady, or Mom always loved you best

THE FACT: It's not easy being the little brother, especially when your big sib is a self-made emperor. So it's no wonder relations between Lucien Bonaparte and brother Napoléon were often abrasive and strained.

At first a supporter of his big bro, Lucien became disillusioned by what he saw as the betrayal of the French Revolution. Unfortunately, he was sort of the Fredo Corleone of the family, being stupid enough to let a subversive pamphlet he had written fall into the hands of Napoléon's police. Obviously, it strained their relationship even further and made him one of the few Bonapartes who didn't end up king of something. In 1804, Lucien went into exile in Rome, and the pope named him Prince of Canino, largely to annoy Napoléon. Not the brightest move. Napoléon imprisoned the pope in 1809. Lucien on the other hand was America-bound. Captured by the British, he remained a prisoner for several years before returning to a comfortable, Napoléon-free retirement on the Continent.

SLICED BREAD

USEFUL FOR: impressing bakers, inventors, and anyone who loves their bread

KEYWORDS: toast, sandwich, or the best thing since sliced bread

THE FACT: It may get a lot of credit now, but at the time of its debut in 1928, sliced bread received less-than-rave reviews.

Baker and inventor Otto Frederick Rohwedder had spent 15 years perfecting his bread slicer (finally settling on one that wrapped the sliced bread to hold it together as opposed to the hat pins he'd tried earlier), but consumers weren't quick to convert. People found the sliced bread strange and senseless. In fact, it wasn't until the advent of Wonder bread, and the collective realization that sliced bread worked better in the toaster, that Rohwedder's invention really took off. By World War II, the military was using sliced bread to serve peanut butter and jelly sandwiches as part of soldiers' rations. Previously uncommon, the PB&J gained a loyal following among servicemen, who kept making the sandwich, sliced bread and all, after they came back to the home front.

SLOT MACHINES

(and one man's tireless shenanigans)

USEFUL FOR: trips to Vegas, bachelor parties, and impressing anyone who's ever tried to cheat the system

KEYWORDS: always bet on the house

THE FACT: Working from the back of his TV repair shop, Tommy Glenn Carmichael figured out more than a few ways to take Vegas, and all their slot machines, for a heck of a ride.

Starting in 1980, Carmichael invented, refined, then manufactured devices for cheating slot machines. Tommy's bag of tricks ranged from coins on strings to light wands that blinded machine sensors, fooling them into dropping their coins. Then, for most of two decades, Carmichael and his partners raked in millions of dollars. But his luck finally ran out when federal agents tapped his phone and heard him discussing a new device that would rack up hundreds of credits per minute on slot machines. In 2001, Carmichael was sentenced to about a year in jail, and was ordered to stay out of casinos. In 2003, he told an Associated Press reporter he was developing a new gadget, called "the Protector." It was designed to stop slot cheaters.

EDGAR ALLAN POE was expelled from West Point for "gross neglect of duty," but many accounts tell it slightly more colorfully. After hearing that the mandatory uniform of the day comprised white gloves and belt, Poe showed up to parade duty wearing those two items but little else.

For his first 35 years, **MR. POTATO HEAD** came equipped with a pipe. But in 1987 he kicked the habit with the help of the American Cancer Society (and no doubt, a nagging Mrs. Potato Head).

GEOFFREY CHAUCER was taken prisoner by the French during the Hundred Years' War, and offered back to England for the measly price of 16 pounds.

SOUP

(or how to give a dog a bowl)

USEFUL FOR: chatting up people who love *Fear Factor*, nonvegetarians, mailmen, and cat lovers

KEYWORDS: I hate dogs or I love soup

THE FACT: While you might be hard pressed to find someone who'll eat it, man's best friend makes man's best soup in some parts of the world.

For those of you with iron stomachs (and no fear of the SPCA), the Chinese Bosintang, or dog meat soup, is relatively easy to make, assuming Bowser is agreeable. The soup requires taking strips of dog meat and boiling them in a soy paste. Then vegetables like green onions, taro stalk as well as the herb perilla leaves are added to the mixture, and the broth is brought to a boil. Finally, a sauce made from mashed garlic, red pepper, and ginger is mixed in. Rumor has it that it goes very well with a glass of soju (an Asian liquor). Of course, the dish has a bit of versatility. Rice can be served with the soup or the combination can be mixed together to make sumptuous leftovers or a warm meal the kids can take in their lunch box . . . or a doggie bag. Ugh.

SOUTHERNERS

(and their fisticuffs)

USEFUL FOR: barroom banter, Civil War reenactments, and avoiding fights across the land

KEYWORDS: excuse me

THE FACT: Strangely enough, "cultures of honor"—or societies where it seems essential for men to avenge insults with their knuckles—have been on anthropologists minds for a while, and the South made for an interesting case.

Two University of Michigan researchers decided to see if the U.S. was still split into cultures of honor. They conducted a study in which a man bumps into a male subject in a long hallway and then calls him a derogatory term (one that rhymes with "bass hole"). The result? Men from the South were deemed more likely to throw a punch. And not only were they visibly angrier than their Northern counterparts, but, after the incident, their saliva tested higher for cortisol (associated with stress, anxiety, and arousal) and testosterone (associated with aggression). It's thought that this simply means that Southerners (generally rural) are less accustomed to this type of confrontation and thus react angrily, whereas Northerners (in crowded urban areas) get bumped around and called names on a regular basis.

SPANISH FLY

(great for beetles, a little less so for humans)

USEFUL FOR: barroom banter, locker room chats, and warning anyone looking for happy pills in Chinatown

KEYWORDS: Viagra, aphrodisiac, or any condition that starts with "erectile"

THE FACT: Mention "Spanish fly," and people's thoughts turn to carnal activities. In truth, though "The Fly" isn't a fly at all, but a beetle.

In fact, it's a beetle that produces a compound called cantharidin, an irritant of the urogenital tract. While it isn't an aphrodisiac, "Spanish fly" can produce an erection. It can also pose a serious threat to human health. Luckily, however, it poses no threat to the male pyrochroid beetles, which rely on the stuff for mating purposes. During the mating ritual, the male secretes a gooey substance that the female tastes. Only if she tastes cantharidin does mating become a possibility—a good example of chemical warfare and species survival. The female passes the cantharidin on to her eggs, which are then less appetizing to predators such as ladybugs.

SPOILED MILK

(and a reason to cry over it)

USEFUL FOR: cocktail parties, impressing history buffs, and anytime you're drinking milk

KEYWORDS: Lincoln, sour milk, or expiration date

THE FACT: Strangely enough, one of the unfortunate victims of bad milk was Abraham Lincoln's mother, Nancy Hanks Lincoln, who died of milk sickness in 1818.

The sickness, which actually wiped out many pioneers, had nothing to do with bacteria and everything to do with a cow's diet. When the animals grazed on a plant called snakeroot, people who drank their milk got sick and often died. A naturally occurring substance in the milk called tremetol was converted by human body enzymes into a highly toxic substance. When chemists linked milk sickness to snakeroot early in the twentieth century, farmers were counseled to rid their fields of the plant, and the milk sickness was quickly eliminated.

SQUID

(studs of the animal kingdom)

USEFUL FOR: barroom banter and making small talk at the aquarium

KEYWORDS: endurance, tentacles, or calamari

THE FACT: According to some interesting recent research, the lowly squid has the kind of stamina that could put Sting to shame.

Scientists at Dalhousie University in Halifax, Nova Scotia, have uncovered the bizarre and intricate mating rituals of the squid, a deep water creature, and, once word gets out, the squid is certain to become the talk of the ocean. Squid mating begins with a "circling nuptial dance," where teams of squid continuously circle around spawning beds in an area that can reach 200 meters across. At daybreak, the squid (or squids, whichever you prefer) begin to mate and continue all day long, halting the activity only long enough for the female to dive down and deposit her eggs. Once she comes back to the circling area, she reunites with her male companion and the process begins again. At dusk, the males and females go offshore to feed and rest. Then, at the first sight of sun, they head back to the spawning area and go at it again all day long. In fact, it's believed that this routine can last for up to two weeks, which undoubtedly results in some sore tentacles.

THE STAR-SPANGLED BANNER

(and the beer it should make you want to chug)

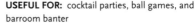

USEFUL FOR: cocktail parties, ball games, and barroom banter

KEYWORDS: will you please stand for . . .

THE FACT: Believe it or not, the American national anthem, and the source of a lot of pre-game pride, was actually nicked from a drinking song written by John Stafford Smith.

Every third-grader knows the story of Francis Scott Key penning the great poem while watching the siege of Fort McHenry during the War of 1812. But that's just a poem. So where exactly did all this music hoo-ha come from? When Key wrote the anthem, he had a song in his head as a reference for the poem's meter (a song from *England*, ironically enough). The tune, notoriously difficult to sing, is from a drinking song written by John Stafford Smith. Original title: "To Anacreon in Heaven." It was the theme song of a club of rich London men who got together to eat, drink, and then for good measure drink some more. The Anacreontic Club took its name from Anacreon, a Greek poet who wrote about such things. Perhaps it's fitting, then, that the song is usually sung before sporting events, after fans have been tailgating (translation: drinking) for several hours.

STELLA (THE FELLA?)

USEFUL FOR: Olympic banter, half-time conversation, and awkward pauses at drag shows and high school track competitions

KEYWORDS: Olympics, track-and-field, or hermaphrodites

THE FACT: In one of the most unusual cases ever, Olympic superstar Stella Walsh was unmasked after her death as being a little more than just woman.

In 1980, a 69-year-old member of the U.S. Track and Field Hall of Fame was shot and killed outside a Cleveland shopping mall. Police immediately ascertained that the victim was Stella Walsh, the greatest female track-and-field athlete of her day. Stella, born Stanislawa Walasiewiczowna in Poland, won a gold medal for Poland at the 1932 Olympics and a silver in 1936, and set 20 world records. But when the police took the body to be autopsied, they found something very unusual on the 69-year-old woman: male genitals! Further studies showed that she had both male and female chromosomes, a condition known as mosaicism. When the shocking news got out, it took approximately 2.7 seconds for the great runner to get a new nickname: Stella the Fella.

SUDDEN DEATH

(leading to sudden death)

USEFUL FOR: cocktail parties, barroom banter, and irritating the sports fans at the retirement home

KEYWORDS: this one's going to go into overtime

THE FACT: If Grandpa's got a heart condition, maybe he shouldn't be watching the big game this week.

Scientists at Utrecht University in the Netherlands analyzed the incidence of death on the five days prior to, the day of, and the five days after semifinal between the Netherlands and France in soccer. The game was particularly exciting, going into overtime before being decided by penalty kicks. (France ultimately won.) The average number of male deaths in the Netherlands by heart attack or stroke on the days surrounding the match: 150; on the day of the match: 173. It isn't known what the French death rate was during and after the match. Guess that means they'll have to do more research.

TELEGRAPH

(the thing Morse didn't invent)

USEFUL FOR: impressing history buffs, irritating anyone related to Sam Morse, and chatting with anyone who still sends telegraphs (if you can find 'em)

KEYWORDS: Morse code, SOS, or how do you type SOS in Morse code?

THE FACT: Forget what you learned in grade school: Samuel F.B. Morse was at the least a second placer when it came to the telegraph.

Instead, set your sights on the true champ, Sir Charles Wheatstone. The British inventor built the first practical electric telegraph in 1837 or 1838—at the very least four years before Morse received his U.S. patent. Even in America, though, Morse's "invention" of the telegraph is fraught with controversy: a friend, Dr. Charles Jackson, accused the inventor of stealing his idea (which could move Morse from second into third place). Also in dispute is the extent to which Morse's assistant, Alfred Vail, contributed to both the design of his telegraph machine and the development of the "Morse code," which was originally called the "Morse-Vail code." (Does that even leave Sammy in the running anymore?) Well, whatever the case, you can always trust that the telegraph system will forever bear the good old Morse name.

TELEPROMPTERS

(and the guy behind it)

USEFUL FOR: making small talk with speechwriters, chatting up politicians, and anytime you see someone squinting at the camera

KEYWORDS: please stay tuned for a message from the president

THE FACT: Talk about an unsung hero: newscasters and politicians everywhere should be on their hands and knees thanking Irving B. Kahn, the inventor of the teleprompter.

Kahn stumbled into the idea while working on a projection system for the U.S. Army (not as a piece of military equipment, but simply to make presentations to Congressmen). Ridding newscasters of the need to read cue cards, the TelePrompTer was a huge success, leading Kahn to start the TelePrompTer Corporation, and leaving us to forever wonder both why newscasters still insist on shuffling papers and why he felt the need to capitalize the *P* and *T* in the company name. But those eternal questions aren't the only annoying legacies Kahn left the world. In 1961, Kahn and fellow TelePrompTer exec Hub Schlafley developed the first pay-per-view television system, called Key TV, by showing (and charging for) the second Patterson – Johansson heavyweight fight.

TELEVISION

(and the kid responsible for must-see TV)

USEFUL FOR: chatting with nerds, scientists, disgruntled inventors, and anyone who used to hang out with the A/V kids

KEYWORDS: television, genius, or unsung hero

THE FACT: Who knew the idea for a TV set came from a 21-year-old Idaho farm boy?

Philo T. Farnsworth took his inspiration from the lines in the freshly tilled fields, and single-handedly dreamed up the cathode ray tube, itself leading to the invention of the television. By scanning and transmitting images in horizontal lines, the young eccentric pioneered an entirely new medium. Sadly, though, his claim to fame was quietly usurped. At just 21, Farnsworth presented his research to RCA executive David Sarnoff and Russian scientist Vladimir Zworykin. Zworykin and Sarnoff then replicated the technology and revised it. Using their position and resources at RCA, the two then began to dominate the marketing of this new technology. Farnsworth sued and seemingly won in court, but the power of the corporation proved mightier, and Farnsworth was never able to profit from the industry he helped launch.

THALES OF MILETUS

(the original Baby Jessica)

USEFUL FOR: cocktail parties, wishing wells, and consoling anyone who's just tripped or fallen

KEYWORDS: Jack and Jill, absentminded, or genius

THE FACT: Thales of Miletus, the first Western philosopher, set the standard for absentminded professors to come. After all, lost in thought and gazing at the sky, Thales fell into a well years before Baby Jessica could make the practice famous.

Of course, the whole well incident wasn't great for PR. Ridiculed as an impractical dreamer, Thales set out to show that philosophers could do anything they set their minds to, including amassing wealth. One winter, using his knowledge of meteorology and astronomy, Thales predicted a bumper olive crop for the coming season. As such, he cornered the market on olive presses in Miletus and made a fortune when the olive harvest met his expectations. Remarkably also, Thales predicted the solar eclipse of 585 BCE. And he measured the height of the Egyptian pyramids using just their shadows. Despite all this, Thales is perhaps best known for arguing that water is the basic source element, that ultimately all things are made of water.

instant personalities

As a practical joke, **JACOB HAUGAARD** promised voters better weather, used his campaign money to buy them franks and beer, and maintained that every man had the God-given right to impotence. He received 23,211 votes, and became the first independent in Denmark's parliament.

In 1820, **LUDWIG VAN BEETHOVEN** was arrested on vagrancy charges after alarmed residents reported a disheveled man peeping in their windows.

STEPHEN STILLS, of the legendary folk-rock group Crosby, Stills & Nash, originally wanted to be a Monkee. His tryout didn't last too long, though, because producers quickly gave his thinning hair and bad teeth two opposable thumbs-down.

TOADS

(and why you should just say no)

USEFUL FOR: mainly warning teenagers and Grateful Dead fans

KEYWORDS: tripping, peer pressure, or Mr. Toad's Wild Ride

THE FACT: No matter what the hype, don't ever lick a cane toad.

In the 1930s "sugar cane" toads were introduced into Australia from Hawaii with the idea that they would control the gray-backed cane beetle, a sugar cane pest. Somehow, though, they became guests that overstayed their welcome—overpopulating and growing to be a real nuisance. Aside from their talent for consuming gray-backed cane beetles, "cane toads" can secrete a toxic compound known as bufotenin from a couple of glands behind their eyes (when attacked by predators, of course). But the toxic goo is also a hallucinogen, albeit a dangerous one. In their endless quest to get high, Australian teenagers have taken to drinking the slime produced when toads are boiled. Clearly, emulating this behavior isn't the brightest idea, as two Canadian kids learned. They purchased a couple of toads from an exotic pet store and licked them hoping for euphoria. They got hospital beds instead.

TWINKIES

(and the law)

USEFUL FOR: cocktail parties, afternoon snack conversation, and chatting up lawyers fond of vending machines

KEYWORDS: Twinkies, insanity, or the law

THE FACT: What should've been an open-and-shut case of murder in the first got a little twisted when a box of Twinkies came to the defense.

There wasn't much question it was Dan White who climbed through a window at San Francisco City Hall and methodically shot to death Mayor George Moscone and Supervisor Harvey Milk, one of the nation's most prominent gay politicians. So lawyers for White, who was an ex-cop and county supervisor, relied on a "diminished capacity" defense. They argued White was too depressed to commit premeditated murder. As proof, they briefly mentioned White's recent consumption of sugary snack foods. Oddly enough, the "Twinkie defense" worked, and White was convicted of manslaughter instead of murder. The verdict, however, triggered a night of rioting in the city's gay community. White served five years in prison and then killed himself a few months after his release. In 1982, California voters abolished diminished capacity as a legal defense.

UNENVIABLE PREGNANCIES

(like the spiny dogfish)

USEFUL FOR: barroom banter, making friends at Lamaze, and ensuring you don't get invited up "for coffee" after a date

KEYWORDS: What could be worse than getting pregnant?

THE FACT: Forget Lamaze! If you want to ease the pain of childbirth, just focus on a spiny dogfish shark.

To conceive, the male spiny dogfish shark grasps the female's fins with his mouth and uses his two reproductive organs, known as clappers, to inseminate the female. But this is no gentle act of foreplay. The sharp clappers leave deep cuts and gashes behind the females head, which take a week or so to heal. Once that's over, she's got a glorious 22 to 24 months of pregnancy to look forward to—the longest gestation period of any vertebrate. And when that magical day finally arrives, you'd better believe she's wondering where *her* epidural is. Spiny dogfish mommies give birth to between two and *eleven* three-foot-long pups, each coming out headfirst. Of course, evolution has equipped the pups with cartilaginous sheaths on their spines to protect the mother from injury. Yeah, like that makes up for it.

UNSHELLED NUTS

(specifically cashews)

USEFUL FOR: cocktail parties, barroom banter, and scaring kids into picking out all the other mixed nuts

KEYWORDS: shell shock, Shell station, or Shelley Long

THE FACT: Cashews aren't sold in shells . . . and there's a darn good reason for it!

While pecans, walnuts, and the oh-so-easy-to-eat pistachios can be shelled with relative ease, their brother the cashew is a nut that's slightly harder to crack. In fact, if you got one in the shell, you'd be struggling to get it out for a good while. Why, exactly? Well, aside from the two layers of shell on the cashew nut, there's also a slightly trickier toxic oil that contains anacardic acid and cardol that can cause blisters on the hands if touched. Cashews have to be roasted twice to be eaten—once to remove the outer shell, and again to remove the inner shell. So do you want 'em au natural and in their shells or all soft and ready to eat like we do?

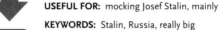

USSR

(and its Tower to the People)

USEFUL FOR: mocking Josef Stalin, mainly

KEYWORDS: Stalin, Russia, really big swimming pools

THE FACT: In 1931, Joseph Stalin ordered that the largest Orthodox Christian cathedral in the world be dynamited so he could build an enormous "Palace of the People." The dynamiting was the easy part.

Wishing to replace the 355-foot-high church—the product of 44 years of backbreaking labor by Russian peasants—with a new structure taller than the Empire State Building, and capped with a gilded statue of Lenin taller than the Statue of Liberty, the "Man of Steel's" mad scheme never came to fruition. The construction on the tower, meant to celebrate Communism's strength, never took place because resources were diverted to fighting World War II. Stalin's successor—Nikita Khrushchev—ordered a large swimming pool built where the cathedral had stood. Old women who remembered the original cathedral could be seen standing at the edge of the swimming pool, praying to forgotten icons. Recently, Yuri Luzhkov, Moscow's autocratic mayor, tried to make up for Stalin's mess by ordering the construction of a tacky reproduction of the original cathedral using precast concrete.

VACUUM CLEANERS

USEFUL FOR: impressing inventors and diverting the conversation when you've been told to clean the carpets

KEYWORDS: chores, chump, or challenge

THE FACT: Forget Hoover. The real guy you should be thanking for the vacuum cleaner is a genius named Hubert Booth.

Hubert Cecil Booth was an Englishman who was always up for a challenge. In 1900, Booth saw a prototype of a dust-removing machine at London's Empire Music Hall and suspected that he could improve on the idea. That wasn't terribly surprising, considering that the machine was designed to force a blast of compressed air down, causing the dust to rise, which might have removed dust from one particular spot on the floor, but not necessarily the room. Predictably, this was somewhat inefficient. When Booth asked the machine's inventor why it just didn't suck *up* the dirt, the man became furious and told him that a machine like that just couldn't be built. Challenge on! Booth started with a few suction experiments, and one short year later he patented the world's first mechanical vacuum.

VACUUMS

(you could never afford)

USEFUL FOR: cocktail parties and small talk while ring shopping

KEYWORDS: vacuum cleaner, Hoover, or Dust Buster

THE FACT: What's the most expensive material, per pound, in common use by physicists. Diamonds? Not even close.

Gem-quality diamonds cost only about $15 million per pound. It's been estimated that Saddam Hussein was willing to spend $100 million per pound for weapons-grade uranium. But that isn't it, either. Moon dust? Nope. Russian-retrieved moon dust (they had a robot return some) has been sold on the black market for less than $5 million per pound. Believe it or not, the most expensive substance per pound is an ultrahigh vacuum. Although it's abundant in space, nobody has figured out a good way to bring them down to earth. The cost of making one is $4 followed by 21 zeros, so nothing else even comes close. And the price will only get more expensive, per gram, as the vacuums get better!

VAN HALEN

(and the whole M&M thing)

USEFUL FOR: cocktail parties and chatting up rock and roll fans and entertainment lawyers

KEYWORDS: prima donnas, egotistical contract agreements, or candy-coated shells

THE FACT: Over the years, Van Halen's gained a lot of notoriety for their demand that at every gig their dressing room had to contain a large bowl of M&Ms with all the brown ones removed. It was for a better reason than you think, though.

While the fact has often been cited as proof of the band members' towering egos, it was actually included by the tour promoters as an easy way of seeing if the concert venues had read the contract thoroughly (particularly the parts about technical requirements, etc.). But sneaky M&M tactics aside, Van Halen's riders are also notorious for the sheer volume of alcohol they stipulate. One rider specified that their dressing room was to contain a case of beer, a pint of Jack Daniels, a pint of Absolut, a 750 ml. bottle of Bacardi Añejo rum, three bottles of wine, small bottles of Cointreau and Grand Marnier, and a 750 ml. bottle of one of five specific premium tequilas. Don't forget six limes, margarita salt, shot glasses, ingredients for Bloody Marys, and a blender.

VELCRO

USEFUL FOR: impressing preschool teachers, scientists, or any six-year-old with shoes

KEYWORDS: natural inventions, inspiration, or cockleburs

THE FACT: The idea for Velcro, one of the greatest inventions in the world (at least for anyone whose ever struggled with tying their laces), started as a thorn in someone's side, literally!

Isaac Newton beneath the apple tree. Archimedes shouting "Eureka!" in the bathtub. And Georges de Mestral going for a walk in the woods. The greatest discoveries often stem from mundane observations, and while gravity (Newton) and measurable density (Archimedes) are cool and everything, nothing beats the sweet music of parting Velcro. Mestral, a Swiss engineer, returned home after a walk in 1948 to find cockleburs stuck to his coat. After examining one under a microscope, he noted that cockleburs attach to clothes and fur via thin hooks. Eureka! It took de Mestral eight years to develop his product. But in the end, the twin nylon strips worked precisely like a cocklebur on a coat—one strip features burlike hooks and the other thousands of small loops to which they attach, forming an unusually sticky bond.

VELVET REVOLUTION

(Czechoslovakia's Quiet Riot)

USEFUL FOR: impressing your history teacher, chatting up rebels or revolutionaries, and instigating shy rabble-rousers the world over

KEYWORDS: velvet, silky smooth, and revolution

THE FACT: Few people believe that the pen is mightier than the sword. Václav Havel and his bloodless revolution might be the best argument for it.

This brave poet and playwright was jailed repeatedly in the 1970s for writing works critical of the communist government in then-Czechoslovakia. With civil unrest rising, he was jailed in February 1989, but kept turning out influential plays, poems, and essays, and even winning literary awards. Set free in May, he helped stoke a peaceful resistance movement known as "the Velvet Revolution." Havel became the focal point of a largely peaceful revolution, where large crowds of nonviolent demonstrators showed their disapproval of the ruling communists. Havel addressed crowds that sometimes numbered almost a million. By the end of the year, the communist government was out and Havel had been elected president. He served as president of Czechoslovakia—and later, when the country split in two, of the Czech Republic—for 13 years, retiring in 2003. The tally? Poetry 1, communism 0!

VODKA

(as in chugging way too much of it)

USEFUL FOR: barroom banter, killing other people's buzzes, and chatting up teetotalers

KEYWORDS: I am soooo drunk right now

THE FACT: Sure, there are beer-drinking contests, so why not vodka-drinking contests? Well, here's why.

In 2003 a bar in the southern Russian town of Volgodonsk decided to hold just such a competition. After all, Russians are famous for their ability to hold their vodka, and annual consumption is over 15 liters *per person*. The winner would get...well, more vodka. Ten liters of it, to be exact. Sadly, the winner never got to claim his prize. After downing 1.5 *liters* of vodka in under 40 minutes (which is about 51 shots) the vodka champ passed away, about 20 minutes later. What about the runners-up? The five other contestants got treated to full luxury stays in intensive care. Scarily enough, many of the ones who weren't hospitalized actually showed up at the same bar the next night.

W. C. FIELDS

USEFUL FOR: cocktail parties, barroom banter, and anywhere that liquor and film buffs pleasantly mix

KEYWORDS: W. C. Fields, chickadee, or I'll drink to that

THE FACT: Of all the alcoholic comedians, the bulbous-nosed W. C. Fields (né William Claude Dukenfield) was by far the least embarrassed by his indulgence.

Fields started his career as a juggler, but found fame with his impeccable wit and comic timing, first on Broadway and then in the movies. Although also noted for his dislike of children ("Any man who hates children and dogs can't be all bad") and his ostentatious immorality (he claimed to religiously study the Bible—in search of loopholes), Fields is probably best known for his drinking. At his peak, Fields downed two *quarts* of gin daily. "I like to keep a bottle of stimulant handy in case I see a snake, which I also keep handy," he once remarked. Fields died on his least favorite of days—Christmas—in 1946.

instant personalities

V is for **VOLKSWAGEN**: Before the first *The Love Bug* film, Disney had a casting call that included Volvos, Toyotas, and about a dozen or so friendly-looking cars. When the staff inspected them, they'd kick tires, grab steering wheels, and roughhouse each one a bit. But when they came to the Beetle, they just began to pet it! The smug car landed the part immediately.

Is **MICKEY MOUSE** married to Minnie? Walt Disney was always coy on the issue. In 1933, he insisted that, in private life, Mickey is married to Minnie, although on-screen, her role is leading lady. Two years later, he proclaimed there is no marriage in the land of make-believe.

CHARLIE CHAPLIN once entered a Charlie Chaplin look-alike contest in a theater in San Francisco, and lost.

WAR
(on drugs)

USEFUL FOR: cocktail parties and impressing your history teacher (as well as the kids who never attended his class)

KEYWORDS: Nazis, cocaine, chewing gum with a kick

THE FACT: As strange as it sounds, during World War II Nazi Germany definitely led the pack in its use of amphetamines, cocaine, and other "performance-enhancing" drugs.

In fact, amphetamine pills were included in every German soldier's first-aid kit, and Nazi researchers developed chewing gum that delivered a dose of cocaine with each piece. But that wasn't all! According to a book by German author and criminologist Wolf Kemper on the subject, *Nazis on Speed*, one of the compounds tested by the Nazis in 1944, D-IX, was actually a cocaine-based compound that included both amphetamine and a morphine-related chemical to dull pain. The experimental drug was tested on prisoners of war, and Nazi doctors found the test subjects could march 55 miles without a rest before they collapsed. The Nazis hoped that the drug could put some fighting spirit into their armies, which were by that time being defeated on all fronts, but luckily the war ended before production could begin.

WEBSTER

(the one behind the dictionary)

USEFUL FOR: chatting up librarians and copy editors, and making friends at the spelling bee

KEYWORDS: Webster, dictionary, spell-checker

THE FACT: Noah Webster was never fondly referred to as "The Godfather of Spelling," but he did offer Americans a spelling (and pronunciation!) resource they couldn't refuse.

A schoolteacher, Webster started out writing spelling books, which soon blossomed into an obsession with standardizing American spelling and pronunciation and distinguishing it from the British. During the 20 years it took him to compile the 70,000-word *American Dictionary of the English Language*, published in 1828, Webster was strongarming prefixes and suffixes in a constant attempt to break words to his own will. He forced *musick* to *music*, carefully urged (for its own good) *centre* to *center*, and—although there were no witnesses to it— changed *plough* to *plow* and *colour* to *color*. Unfortunately, he was so busy instilling order and structure to the language that he never got around to changing words like *bureaucracy* to something a little more phonetically friendly.

WEDDING TRADITIONS

(and why you can't see your bride)

USEFUL FOR: bridal showers, blind dates, and wedding receptions

KEYWORDS: here comes the bride

THE FACT: It's a common American tradition: Keep the glowing bride in hiding on the morning of her wedding so that the groom can be all the more awestruck by the sight of his woman in white. Sounds sweet, but its origins aren't quite so tender.

For hundreds of years, fathers arranged the marriages of their daughters by offering money to young men. However, if Daddy's Little Girl wasn't exactly fit for the cover of *Maxim*, Daddy might decide to search for prospective grooms in nearby towns, for obvious reasons. When these men showed up on their wedding day—not having seen their future bride before—it was common for some of them to flee the scene. So the tradition that it's "bad luck" for a man to see his bride before the ceremony really started out as just insurance for her dad.

WEREWOLF SYNDROME

USEFUL FOR: barroom banter, Halloween chatter, and making small talk with the person waxing your back

KEYWORDS: hairy, hairball, or Henderson

THE FACT: Forget your cousin Sal and his hirsute offspring, the Ramos Gomez clan of Mexico currently holds the Guinness record for world's hairiest family.

Five generations of this family's members suffer from hypertrichosis, or "werewolf syndrome," which causes thick hair to grow over the entire body (98 percent of it, to be exact), including the face, ears, and neck. Brothers Larry and Danny Ramos Gomez are the most well known of the family, as they travel the world performing their duties as professional trampoline acrobats—an occupation no doubt made appealing by the fact that it's actually weirder than having hair all over your face. But Larry and Danny wanted a profession that wasn't contingent on their appearance. In the 1990s, producers at the *The X-Files* offered them guest-starring roles, but they declined.

WHITE-FRONTED PARROTS

USEFUL FOR: cocktail parties, nerdy dates, and proving that Polly doesn't want a chauvinist

KEYWORDS: birds, chicks, or sensitive males

THE FACT: White-fronted parrots are something of an anomaly in the animal kingdom. For one thing, they may be the only species (besides humans) to engage in what is essentially the act of "kissing"!

Before mating, the male and female birds will lock beaks and gently flick their tongues together. If that goes well, the males will make the bold move for "second base," which involves regurgitating food for his mate in a generous show of affection. How sweet! Native to Mexico and Central America, white-fronted parrots were also totally ahead of us with the whole "two-income marriage" deal. Along with various species of the albatross, penguin, ostrich, and other large birds, white-fronted parrots generally lay a solitary egg, with both the male and the female taking turns incubating it. Once the chick hatches, both parents feed and otherwise care for the young bird.

WOODCHUCKS

(and how much wood they chuck)

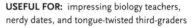

USEFUL FOR: impressing biology teachers, nerdy dates, and tongue-twisted third-graders

KEYWORDS: Woodchuck cider, Groundhog Day, or beavers

THE FACT: So how much wood would a woodchuck chuck? Probably none.

Woodchucks aren't particularly tree-oriented, and while they can climb to find food, they prefer being on the ground. In fact, they actually got the name "woodchuck" from British trappers who couldn't quite wrap their tongues around the Cree Indian name, "wuchak." More commonly (and accurately) known as groundhogs, these animals are closely related to squirrels, marmots, and prairie dogs, with whom they share an affinity for burrowing. And while they aren't so prone to chucking wood, a burrowing woodchuck *can* chuck dirt, in the form of tunnels that can reach five feet deep and as much as 35 feet in length. Based on that number, New York State wildlife expert Richard Thomas calculates that, if a woodchuck could chuck wood, it could chuck as much as 700 pounds of the stuff.

WORK

(you probably don't want)

USEFUL FOR: seafood buffets, barroom banter, and realizing how much better your job is than you know

KEYWORDS: Alaska, fishermen, or king crab special

THE FACT: Annoying bosses, bad benefits, and even preretirement pink slips can't make a job more hellish than that of Alaskan king crab fishermen.

Because most crab are harvested during the winter months in Alaska, conditions are particularly brutal, with strong winds, short daylight hours, and high seas. Every year, 34 fishing vessels and 24 lives are lost in the water around Alaska—an occupational fatality rate 20 times the national average. Most deaths result from hypothermia, capsizing, or falling overboard. The risks are exacerbated by exhaustion, because the fishermen often work 20-hour shifts pulling 450-pound crab cages across the slippery deck. But the hard work pays off—if you survive. Alaskan king crab fishermen work for shares of their vessel, with some boats bringing in $200,000 a day, and deckhands taking home up to $100,000 in a four-month season.

WORLD WAR III

(as almost started by a bear)

USEFUL FOR: impressing your history teacher, terrifying your friends, and occasionally as a fun fact whenever you're watching Yogi Bear cartoons

KEYWORDS: Cuban Missile Crisis, nuclear holocaust, or the Bad News Bears

THE FACT: On October 25, 1962, during the Cuban Missile Crisis, a security guard at an airbase in Duluth, Iowa, saw a shadowy figure scaling one of the fences enclosing the base. It almost led to a world war.

The guard shot at the intruder and activated an intruder alarm, automatically setting off intruder alarms at neighboring bases. However, at the Volk Field airbase in Wisconsin, the Klaxon loudspeaker had been wired incorrectly, and instead sounded an alarm ordering F-106A interceptors armed with nuclear missiles to take off. The pilots presumed that a full-scale nuclear conflict with the Soviet Union had begun, and the planes were about to take off when a car from the air traffic control tower raced down the tarmac and signaled the planes to stop. The intruder in Duluth had finally been identified: it was a bear.

THE WORST

(a guy named Napoleon)

USEFUL FOR: cocktail parties, academic gatherings, and making friends with a Yanomami

KEYWORDS: Napoleon, anthropology, or "I've never had the measles"

THE FACT: Until 2000, Napoleon Chagnon was known as author of the best-selling anthropology text of all time: *Yanomamö: The Fierce People*. But since then his so-called research has been mired in controversy.

The anthropologist, along with geneticist James Neel, inoculated many of the Venezuelan tribe's members against measles. Unfortunately, it was right about this time that the Yanomami experienced their first-ever measles epidemic, leading to thousands of deaths and reducing the tribe to half its original size. Coincidence? Perhaps. Many defend the expedition, claiming it would be impossible for a vaccine to spark such an outbreak. Critics point to the expedition's financier, the Atomic Energy Commission, as proof that the accused were using the Yanomami as human test subjects. Either way, the scandal raised serious questions about the practices of studying indigenous peoples, and made it nearly impossible for Neel and Chagnon to pick up ladies at future anthropological conventions.

WRIGHT

('cause when you're Wright, you're Wright)

USEFUL FOR: housewarming parties, chatting up architects, and irritating fans of Frank Lloyd Wright

KEYWORDS: temper tantrum, prima donna, or *Trading Spaces*

THE FACT: Whether or not Frank Lloyd Wright could walk on water, the genius designer behind Fallingwater sort of believed he could.

It's true, the amazing designer of the Robie House, Fallingwater, Taliesin West, the Guggenheim Museum, and countless other buildings was notorious for his belief in his superiority to mere mortals. In fact, the architectural egomaniac frequently acted as if the rules did not apply to him—even the rules of geography and climate. But when you're Wright, your Wright. Commissioned in 1935 to design a Dallas home for department store magnate Stanley Marcus, the project quickly went sour when he insisted that his client sleep outdoors year-round on "sleeping porches." He also decreed that the Marcus small bedroom "cubicles" would have almost no closet space. When Stan respectfully explained that a) it is frequently well over 90 degrees at night during Dallas summers and b) a high-fashion tastemaker might need bigger closets, Wright threw a series of tantrums in letters still extant that make for delicious reading.

XIUHCÓATL

(and the wrathful god that wielded it)

USEFUL FOR: scaring kids, impressing mass murderers, and making conversation during the Kali Ma scenes of *Indiana Jones and the Temple of Doom*

KEYWORDS: Aztec, sacrifices, or the phrase "show a little heart"

THE FACT: The ambition of the Aztec empire might well be linked to one wrathful god and his turquoise snake.

According to Aztec legend, Huitzilopochtli's 401 older siblings tried to kill him, but the clever god turned the tables on them and wiped 'em out with his weapon of choice, the xiuhcóatl (or for those of you who don't speak Aztec, a turquoise snake). Represented either as a hummingbird or as a warrior with armor and helmet made of hummingbird feathers (not exactly bulletproof), Huitzilopochtli was both God of the Sun and the God of War. As such, Aztecs believed that he needed a steady diet of human hearts—preferably of the warrior variety—and human blood. In fact, the need to feed Huitzilopochtli fueled the Aztecs' ambition, and increased their urgency for fighting and conquering other peoples.

X-DRESSING

(for success)

USEFUL FOR: cocktail parties, classical performances, and making small talk at drag shows and divorce procedures

KEYWORDS: jealousy, cross-dressing, or Berlioz

THE FACT: Luckily for the world, French composer Hector Berlioz was fished out of the Mediterranean. Unluckily for Berlioz, he was wearing women's clothing at the time.

The renowned musician Hector Berlioz was, among other things, wacky. While away in Rome studying on a scholarship, he heard that his beloved girlfriend, Camille, back in Paris, had started seeing another guy. Furious, he resolved to kill his rival. But he needed to disguise himself. So he bought a gun, put on a dress, and boarded a train for Paris. Halfway home, however, Berlioz chickened out and threw himself into the Mediterranean. Thankfully for the world, and for music, he was fished out (minus the gun).

X-ROADS

(where to sell your soul for the blues)

USEFUL FOR: cocktail parties, barroom banter, and jazz club discussions

KEYWORDS: Robert Johnson, the devil, or how the hell can someone be that good

THE FACT: According to some folk, there's only one way to get as good as Robert Johnson did—by making a pact with the devil.

Considered the most influential bluesman of all time, Robert Johnson is also one of the most turbulent. And few musicians have achieved Johnson's mythical status, whether the devil had a hand in it or not. As the story goes, one night Johnson happened upon a large black man walking near the crossroads of Highways 61 and 49 outside of Clarksdale, Mississippi. The man offered to tune Johnson's guitar, and claimed Johnson's soul in return. Within a year, Johnson was in demand throughout the region. Actually, the story may have started when Johnson sat in on a gig with Sun House and Willie Brown. House and Brown were so impressed with Johnson's playing they thought the only explanation was that he'd sold his soul. Of course, mythic lives require mythic endings. Known for his womanizing, Johnson was fatally poisoned when he sipped some whiskey laced with strychnine—the act of a jealous husband.

THE YAP

(currency for a rockier time)

USEFUL FOR: cocktail parties, chatting up a world traveler, and joking with your teller

KEYWORDS: too much change, bulky wallet, or hernia

THE FACT: If you're frustrated by the market, and you're looking for a currency that can stand the test of time, look no further.

In the Caroline Islands in the South Pacific, there's an island named Yap (or Uap). In 1903, an American anthropologist named Henry Furness III visited the islanders and found they had an unusual system of currency. It consisted of carved stone wheels called *fei*, ranging in diameter from a foot to 12 feet. Because the stones were heavy, the islanders didn't normally carry their money around with them. After a transaction, the *fei* might remain on a previous owner's premises, but it was understood who owned what. One family's *fei*, Furness was told, had been lost at sea many years earlier while being transported from a nearby island during a storm. But that stone was still used as currency, even though it was unseen and irretrievable beneath hundreds of feet of water.

YEMEN'S NATIONAL PASTIME

USEFUL FOR: barroom banter, impressing locals wherever finer nicotine and drug paraphernalia are sold

KEYWORDS: dip, chewing tobacco, or national pastime

THE FACT: Believe it or not, the national obsession of Yemen is basically chewing a mild stimulant known as qat.

Every afternoon, much of Yemen simply shuts down as men gather together to chew great wads of qat and convivially discuss events. A few writers have gone so far as to blame Yemen's persistent poverty on the drug, largely because chewing it simply eats up so much time. A more reasonable concern is that qat cultivation is undermining Yemen's agriculture, because other crops are being abandoned in favor of the much more profitable drug. Yemen was once the world's major supplier of coffee, but those days are long gone. The Yemenis evidently think that they have found a better stimulant, even if most of the rest of the world begs to differ.

ZAMBONI

(and its best hood ornament)

USEFUL FOR: cocktail parties, dates at the aquarium, and stirring up conversation at a sushi dinner

KEYWORDS: octopus, Red Wings, or pimp my ride

THE FACT: Everyone knows that octopi can really touch up a Zamboni at the center of an ice rink or add just a hint of pizzazz when fashionably draped from the rafters. At least anyone who's ever been to a Detroit hockey game.

If you're looking for more tips in mollusk décor, though, you'll actually need to head out to one of the Red Wings' games for yourself, where you'll be sure to find 20 to 30 octopi displayed on the ice. Why, exactly? It's a tradition that started in 1952 during the Red Wings' Stanley Cup run. During the game, fans Jerry and Pete Cusimano tossed a boiled octopus onto the ice—its eight legs symbolic of the Red Wings' eight straight wins (at the time, only eight wins were needed to win the playoffs). The crowd went wild (instead of being confused), and a sports tradition was born. Since then, the largest octopus to land on the ice weighed in at 50 pounds. Later in the game, it was displayed on the hood of the Zamboni while the ice was being cleaned between periods, definitely a hood ornament worth emulating.

ZERO

(as in the number of witches burnt to a crisp)

USEFUL FOR: bonfire banter, Halloween parties, and road-trip chatter en route to Massachusetts

KEYWORDS: witches, Joan of Arc, or Salem, Massachussetts

THE FACT: No matter what impression you've gotten from your high school reading *The Crucible* or bad late night PBS, the truth is there were zero (as in no) witches burned at the stake in New England.

While most people think the witches of Salem were skewered en masse, the truth is that no witches were ever burned during the infamous witch hysteria of 1692. However, this doesn't mean that they didn't have it really, really bad. Of the 150 people accused of witchcraft, only 20 were sentenced to death: 19 of them were hanged; the remaining "witch" was crushed to death by stones. Oh, and six of them were men.

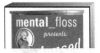